WHAT ARE THE HUMANITIES FOR?

What are the humanities for? The question has perhaps never seemed more urgent. While student numbers have grown in higher education, universities and colleges increasingly have encouraged students to opt for courses in STEM (science, technology, engineering and mathematics) or take programs in applied subjects like business and management. When tertiary learning has taken such a notably utilitarian turn, the humanities are judged to have lost their centrality. Willem B. Drees has no wish nostalgically to prioritize the humanities so as to retrieve some lost high culture. But he does urge us to adopt a clearer conception of the humanities as more than just practical vehicles for profit or education. He argues that these disciplines, while serving society, are also intrinsic to our humanity. His bold ideas about how to think with greater humanistic coherence mark this topical book out as unmissable reading for all those involved in academe, especially those in higher educational policy or leadership positions.

WILLEM B. DREES is a philosopher of the humanities and of religion, a former academic dean, member of the Royal Holland Society of Sciences and Humanities (KHMW), recipient of two Fulbright Grants, and author of *Beyond the Big Bang: Quantum Cosmologies and God* (1990) and *Religion, Science and Naturalism* (1996).

What Are the Humanities For?

WILLEM B. DREES

CAMBRIDGE
UNIVERSITY PRESS

University Printing House, Cambridge CB2 8BS, United Kingdom

One Liberty Plaza, 20th Floor, New York, NY 10006, USA

477 Williamstown Road, Port Melbourne, VIC 3207, Australia

314–321, 3rd Floor, Plot 3, Splendor Forum, Jasola District Centre, New Delhi – 110025, India

79 Anson Road, #06–04/06, Singapore 079906

Cambridge University Press is part of the University of Cambridge.

It furthers the University's mission by disseminating knowledge in the pursuit of education, learning, and research at the highest international levels of excellence.

www.cambridge.org
Information on this title: www.cambridge.org/9781108838412
DOI: 10.1017/9781108974615

First published 2021

Printed in the United Kingdom by TJ Books Ltd. Padstow Cornwall

A catalogue record for this publication is available from the British Library.

Library of Congress Cataloging-in-Publication Data
NAMES: Drees, Willem B., 1954– author.
TITLE: What are the humanities for? / Willem B. Drees, Tilburg University, The Netherlands.
DESCRIPTION: Cambridge ; New York, NY : Cambridge University Press, 2021. | Includes bibliographical references and index.
IDENTIFIERS: LCCN 2020043357 (print) | LCCN 2020043358 (ebook) | ISBN 9781108838412 (hardback) | ISBN 9781108965323 (paperback) | ISBN 9781108974615 (epub)
SUBJECTS: LCSH: Humanities–Philosophy.
CLASSIFICATION: LCC AZ103 .D68 2021 (print) | LCC AZ103 (ebook) | DDC 001.301–dc23
LC record available at https://lccn.loc.gov/2020043357
LC ebook record available at https://lccn.loc.gov/2020043358

ISBN 978-1-108-83841-2 Hardback
ISBN 978-1-108-96532-3 Paperback

Contents

Acknowledgments

In covering a territory as wide as "the humanities," I owe much to all the teachers of my life, to colleagues at home and abroad, to students whose presence and questions stimulated my own development, to donors and taxpayers who support universities and other academic institutions, and to friends, including friends outside the academic world, to whom I owe an explication of our domain. Important to me have been colleagues and students in religious studies at Leiden University, my academic home from 2001 until 2014, and from Leiden's School of Humanities. I want to mention here, in particular, Maghiel van Crevel whose engagement with Area Studies, and hence with humanities in a global context, is inspiring; he directed me to helpful literature on Area Studies.

Philosophically very enriching for me has been the participation in a multi-university research collaboration funded by the Netherlands Organization of Scientific Research (NWO), "What Can the Humanities Contribute to Our Practical Self-Understanding?" initiated by Marcus Düwell of Utrecht University, with Jos de Mul of the Erasmus University Rotterdam and other colleagues and graduate students. On the reflexivity of human self-understanding as central to my working definition of the humanities, I was inspired by my graduate student in this program, Annemarie Van Stee, now at the Radboud University Nijmegen, who titled her PhD thesis *Understanding Existential Self-Understanding: Philosophy Meets Cognitive Neuroscience* (Leiden University, 2017).

As dean of the Tilburg School of Humanities (2015–2018), I am grateful for regular exchanges with fellow deans of other schools in the Netherlands. I am especially grateful for colleagues in the Tilburg School of Humanities; to those who responded to my inaugural address in January 2015, an earlier effort to reflect upon the humanities; to Alkeline van Lenning, dean of University College Tilburg, and Herman de Regt, vice-dean for education, for exchanges on education; to Odile Heynders for exchanges on humanities and digital culture; and to two successive vice-deans for research, Paul Post and Marc Swerts. After I had stepped down from administrative duties, the Department of Philosophy provided me with a new academic home. The invitation by Wim Dubbink, head of the department, to teach various courses, was stimulating, especially an introductory course on the history of modern philosophy, which legitimized reading biographies of Baruch Spinoza and Immanuel Kant and the correspondence between René Descartes and Princess Elisabeth of Bohemia.

A first draft of the present book was written in the spring of 2019 while I was the CTI Distinguished Fellow in the Humanities at the Center of Theological Inquiry in Princeton, NJ, USA. I am very grateful to its director, Will Storrar, and to Joshua Mauldin, its associate director, for the hospitable and stimulating research environment they have created; to its sponsors that keep such a special place alive; and to my fellow fellows for intellectual exchange and stimulus. From among those, I want to mention, in particular, Dirk Evers from the University of Halle-Wittenberg, who reminded me of Adolf Harnack's address and mentioned the difference in pronunciation of the English "to go" and "to do." I am also most grateful to the staff of various libraries, in particular the library of Princeton Theological Seminary, the Firestone Library of Princeton University, and the Public Library of Princeton, and back home to Leiden University Libraries and Tilburg University Library.

I want to express my gratitude to colleagues who have taken precious time to read the initial draft, in part or in full, and provided me with valuable feedback. This includes three reviewers for Cambridge University Press who remained anonymous to me, and Marcus Düwell, Odile Heynders, Arie Molendijk, Jos de Mul, and Marc Swerts. I haven't followed all their advice, and have to accept all the blame for errors and limitations. I also want to express my gratitude toward Beatrice Rehl, senior editor of the Press, and Alex Wright, head of its Humanities division, for their encouragement, and to the Press for accepting this book for publication.

Writing on the humanities is a human effort. Alongside all the academics, including many more who have not been mentioned above by name, I want to mention Zwanet for her continuing presence and support, and our three children and their partners. Also, our grandchildren, new human beings who came into the world in the years while I developed this book, reminding me joyfully of the richness of human existence and the legacies we pass on to future humans, as well as, with shared guilt, of the mess we leave to future generations. I wonder what their world will be like, but I am convinced that in a time of robotics and artificial intelligence, there will be an even greater relevance of human self-reflection and of engagement with others, and hence significance to the humanities.

Canine, Alien, and Human Humanities

An Introduction

DOGS KNOW THEIR HUMANS. THEY RECOGNIZE OUR VOICES, take their cues from our behavior, and sense our emotions. But the canine understanding of humans is limited; they would not be able to understand even a simple text or argument. They lack a language that makes a conceptual world possible. At least, to us, such seems to be doggish existence. Their understanding of humans is limited and instrumental. They know that which is necessary to be fed, walked, and groomed. They know that which is important to keep their humans serving them.

Extraterrestrials, assuming these to exist and to be intelligent, may have a conceptual world. It would be their conceptual world. If aliens were studying life on Earth, their work on humans might be comparable to our zoology and botany, the study of other organisms. In contrast to *canine humanities*, a dog's knowledge of humans, *alien humanities* might be conceptually complex and driven by intrinsic curiosity. But it might well be that those extraterrestrials do not recognize themselves in the humans they study, just as we do not recognize ourselves in the lives of bats in the air or of jelly fish in the seas.

This book is not about such real or imaginary other beings. It is about us, humans. We are humans who relate to fellow humans by using language. We recognize ourselves in movies or stories. We live in a cultural world shaped by the social and legal arrangements we have created. We are humans who interpret our world and attempt to understand our fellow humans and ourselves. This book is about the scholarly study of our human world, which we have come to call "the humanities," the study of the stories and histories, languages and literatures, religions, and moralities of humans. As this is done by humans, rather than by dogs or aliens, this is about *human humanities*.

Knowing the language of others is useful in commerce and war. We may also seek understanding of others for our own benefit, as we can learn from others, and appropriate what is useful to us. But we engage in humanities not only for profit or education, but also because the engagement with others and the self-reflective effort to understand ourselves serves society and is intrinsic to our humanity. In order to envisage such a broader view of what the humanities might be for, we need a vision of what the humanities are.[1]

WHAT ARE THE HUMANITIES?

It may seem to be a rather diverse collection of disciplines, such as history, literary studies, linguistics, area studies, art history, religious studies, philosophy, and more. Perhaps a convenient label in university administration, but not much more. Against such a view, in Chapter 1 I offer a proposal for a tentative definition of the humanities, jointly, as a *coherent* domain. The main ambition here is to explore and understand the nature of the humanities, as human efforts to live with others and understand them, and to understand ourselves and reflect upon our own convictions. They serve to understand others, past and present (Chapter 2), and ourselves, our identities, and arguments (Chapter 3). Though this involves us as humans, and hence our preferences, biases and values, a particular role-specific neutrality should be the ambition; responsible scholarship is the aspiration (Chapter 4).

WHO NEEDS THE HUMANITIES?

This question is central to the second half of this book. In higher education, student numbers have grown. Politically, the push has been

[1] The title What Are the Humanities For?, introduced after completion of the manuscript, is inspired by Stefan Collini, *What Are Universities For?* (London: Penguin Books, 2012). He also writes on the humanities, as these are central to his vision for the universities.

to promote STEM disciplines, Science, Technology, Engineering and Medicine, while many individual students opt for programs with a focus on business and management. The humanities seem to have lost their central place. Some colleagues in the universities are nostalgic about an idealized earlier phase in history when the universities served a limited elite. I do not share such nostalgia, and do not want to prioritize humanities in terms of ideals of "high culture."[2]

What, then, is our place? For whom might it be relevant? For professionals, as we will see in a case study on religious and legal interpretation, with religious fundamentalists and legal originalists claiming to be true to the original meaning (Chapter 5). But the humanities are not only of interest to professionals. The humanities are deeply human, given the material, biological, cultural, technological, and planetary beings we are (Chapter 6). The value of the humanities is multi-facetted. We need the humanities for commercial purposes, for society, and for culture. While the humanities do have public value[3], last but not least they also are valuable in themselves (Chapter 7).

WHY THIS BOOK?

The aim is to envisage the *humanities as a coherent* domain: The humanities appear to be a mixed bag of disciplines and programs, administratively put together but not intrinsically connected. The aim is to think more clearly, and with greater coherence, about the humanities, as a basis for thinking about their public value and intrinsic significance, about quality and relevance.

To students it can be valuable to develop a larger vision of humans and the humanities, and thereby a richer appreciation of their own course of studies. To me, it was important when I became dean, within the school of humanities and when representing the school, and thus

[2] Concern on nostalgia is also voiced by Collini in What Are Universities For?, p. 41, in a chapter on John Henry Newman's *The Idea of a University Defined and Illustrated* (1873).

[3] Justin Bate (ed.), *The Public Value of the Humanities* (London: Bloomsbury, 2011); Paul Benneworth, Magnus Gulbrandsen, and Ellen Hazelkorn, *The Impact and Future of Arts and Humanities Research* (London: Palgrave Macmillan, 2016).

the humanities, in the university and in society, as I needed to be able to say "what we are and why that matters."

It is not only relevant for such introductory, pragmatic, and political purposes. There is also an intellectual need, to think through what the humanities are, how this pursuit is typical of human nature, and how it should be pursued to deliver scholarly quality, despite the biases and values we bring to our studies. As my initial training has been in theoretical physics and mathematics, the question to what extent the humanities are similar to the natural sciences, and why they are different in important ways, is important to me. As I subsequently studied theology and religious studies, and philosophy, I am especially intrigued by the way scholarship and personal engagement interact, and have an impact on identities, beliefs, and practices.

In my reflections on the humanities, I will draw on experiences in the Netherlands and on encounters with colleagues in Europe, North America, and Asia. I never regretted my initial training in physics and mathematics. Some years later, I studied theology at a public university. The academic study of theology is like a square where many streets come together. History, languages, anthropology, psychology, ethics, and philosophy were all part of the curriculum. To study religion, one needs to acquire knowledge of human beliefs and practices. Such a study requires critical reflection on methods and terminology. It also calls for self-reflection, on one's own convictions and biases. The study of religion is a domain where one encounters the humanities in their diversity. My writing is shaped by religious studies, theology, and philosophy, and by my involvement in reflections on their co-existence with the natural sciences.[4]

The present book reflects my subsequent journey into the humanities: A domain that I have found to be more challenging than particle physics, or at least one that turned out to be a challenge of a different kind. It is not easy to pose the right questions. Terminology is often in dispute. Discussions hardly ever result in a definitive conclusion.

[4] Willem B. Drees, *Beyond the Big Bang: Quantum Cosmologies and God* (La Salle, IL: Open Court, 1990); Drees, *Religion, Science and Naturalism* (Cambridge University Press, 1996); Drees, *Religion and Science in Context: A Guide to the Debates* (London: Routledge, 2010); and Willem B. Drees and Pieter Sjoerd van Koningsveld (eds.), *The Study of Religion and the Training of Muslim Clergy in Europe: Academic and Religious Freedom in the 21st Century* (Leiden University Press, 2008).

At the same time, the humanities are fascinating. We consider how humans understand themselves and their communities. How we express ourselves in art and by speaking and writing. How we come to judgments regarding beauty and justice. How culture and social life are changing due to globalization and digitalization. The grander narratives of societies and their histories, and much else.

For me, reflections acquired urgency when involved in academic leadership. I served as dean, first of the school of theology, later religious studies, at Leiden University, and, following a merger, as vice-dean for education in the School of Humanities, overseeing a wide range of programs on languages and cultures from all over the world, both past and present. Some years later, I became dean of the Tilburg School of Humanities, later School of Humanities and Digital Sciences. To develop an academic community, with all the variation there is, one needs a vision, to see each as involved in a larger, coherent effort. My 2015 inaugural address *Naked Ape or Techno Sapiens? The Relevance of Human Humanities* was a preliminary attempt,[5] while this book further develops my reflections on the humanities.

As reflections on the humanities are reflections on humans, and hence, potentially relevant to us all, the following is written for a diverse audience. Among them, I have in mind students, colleagues, and university administrators, but also friends who were trained in other disciplines and pursued other careers. Thus, I intend to avoid as far as I can technical vocabulary. The bibliography lists titles on the general theme. Details on sources regarding particular topics can be found in the notes, but the text should be readable without being interrupted by a need to turn to these notes.

[5] Willem B. Drees, *Naked Ape or Techno Sapiens? The Relevance of Human Humanities* (Tilburg University, 2015).

Part I

What Are the Humanities?

Humanities are academic disciplines in which humans seek understanding of human self-understandings and self-expressions, and of the ways in which people thereby construct and experience the world they live in. Thus, the tentative definition developed in the first chapter. Most humans are "other humans," near and far. To understand these, we need to be able to communicate – and, hence, we need language. And we need to understand their context, their place, the space they move in. As we seek to understand them, we need to reflect upon the process of understanding and the criteria involved. Our scholarly understanding of others need not be received well, as historical insight may be at odds with the self-understanding of people involved. Such topics will be considered in Chapter 2, "Understanding Others."

Humanities are not only about others, but also about ourselves. How should we live? How should we argue and judge? Who are we? This self-involving and self-reflective dimension of the humanities is explicit in philosophy and theology, and central to Chapter 3.

We need more than just opinions; we need knowledge that is not determined by personal preferences but guided by relevant social and epistemic (knowledge-promoting) values. Also, we need ways of constructing knowledge in relation to data, as inductive and hypothetical-deductive schemes in the natural sciences. Last but not least, we need to recognize that the humans studied remain actors, thus challenging the understanding that may have emerged. Such topics are central to Chapter 4, "Responsible Scholarship."

1

The Humanities

We, humans, write text messages, love letters, and manifestos. By our dress we distinguish ourselves from others. By the food we eat, the company we seek, the histories we present as our own, and the stories we tell we express our emotions, attitudes, and beliefs. We create works of art, to convey a message, to make money, or apparently for no reason at all. We do things, by speaking and in other ways. By our actions we shape the lives we live and the social, cultural, and material world we live in. We are actors.

We live in a world shared with others. Others we need to understand, though understanding does not always come easily. We experience others, past and present, as we encounter their art and culture, and thus learn how they present and understand themselves, their identities. This world we share with others has been shaped over time. We haven't started from scratch, but we are, for now, at the receiving end of history, while contributing to its future. History we encounter in the layout of our cities, in the objects we use, in the stories we hear, in the language we speak, in the ideas we have.

As we experience others, we may come to know them, their ways of speaking and acting. Much knowledge is implicit. When learning a second language alongside our mother tongue, we may notice similarities and differences – and thus start to think about the grammatical structure of these languages. So, too, for learning about the historical experiences of others, seeing similarities. Also, differences – the Dutch "Golden Age" appears differently for Dutch "burghers" than for inhabitants of the East Indies, now Indonesia, and differently for sailormen who escaped poverty than for slaves shipped from Africa to the

Americas. By learning the perspectives of others, we may make explicit ideas about our situation that at first were only implicit. What appears to some to be self-evident thus may come to be seen as accidental. To deepen our knowledge of others and of ourselves, some of us go on to study in depth the ways in which humans present and express themselves.

In the *humanities* we study human languages, historical episodes, cultures, artistic expressions, ritual practices, religious beliefs, and much more. We study histories and languages of people far and near, and thereby we come to understand better our own language and history as well. By studying their art and their beliefs, we may come to reconsider our own beliefs and expressions as well. By developing our knowledge of humans, by engaging in the humanities, we learn to navigate this complex world with other humans. We are humans studying humans.

The self-reference of humans studying humans is typical for the humanities. It shows itself very clearly in disciplines such as philosophy or cultural studies. When studying other humans, we may compare their languages, cultures, and experiences to our own experiences in the world. We can learn from studying others. Though we make mistakes and errors as well, as bias and prejudice are human, too. Too often we have also dismissed others; noise made by barbarians was not really language, to draw upon an embarrassing stereotype. When others are treated thus, we thereby do injustice to their humanity by not approaching them as fellow humans who might have to offer something of interest to us.

The elementary take-home message of this book is the following. There is much to be discovered about humans, others and ourselves. This is not merely knowledge about something out there, an object that might be of academic interest. This is knowledge that engages ourselves as persons in relation to others, as we humans are *subjects* who develop such knowledge about *subjects*, about persons who also have an inner life, who experience the world, and who intend to shape their world. Even though the humanities and the natural sciences both seek knowledge, and thus to some extent are similar in kind, the self-reference involved in subjects studying subjects requires an approach that takes all those involved serious as persons. This "subjective" involvement of ourselves as humans who do humanities makes the humanities different from the natural sciences. We are engaged in *human humanities.*

HUMANITIES: A DEFINITION

The humanities include a plurality of scholarly disciplines such as the study of history, languages, religions, and art from various times and places, and, often comparatively, linguistics, literary studies, cultural studies, philosophy, religious studies, and area studies. The word "humanities" appears to be a plural, just as "sciences" is a plural. There are individual sciences, such as chemistry and biology. However, there is no singular form of the humanities that serves as such; one cannot say that art history is "a humanity." In English, "humanity" does not refer to individual disciplines, though in the nineteenth century in some of the ancient Scottish universities there was a professor of Humanity, that is, a professor of Latin.[1] In common parlance today, "humanity" refers to us as a collective, to human beings, the human species, and to human nature. This term has aesthetic and moral weight, when the term stands for "being civilized" or "realizing our full humanity," or when one speaks of crimes against our common humanity.

As the English language is used today, "humanities" suggests a plurality. This plurality fits the humanities well, as the study of humans involves a wide variety of disciplines and approaches, some seeking knowledge that is as objective as feasible, others very sensitive to the way personal assumptions and interests shape the questions we ask and the methods we use. Despite significant diversity within the domain of the humanities, I seek to envisage these disciplines together, treating the humanities as one major domain within our human pursuit of knowledge.

The term "humanities" suggests something universal, applicable in all social and historical contexts, rather than China studies, European studies, American studies, or Classics – each more specific in space or time. In the sense used here, the term became prominent at first in the USA, and, to some extent, still reflects that origin. As an American

1 Stefan Collini, *What Are Universities For?* (London: Penguin, 2012), p. 63.

academic, Geoffrey Galt Harpham, reflecting on lectures he gave at universities in Istanbul, notes,

> I began my visit with the casual presumption that the humanities are a global undertaking that had been advanced with particular success in the United States, I ended convinced that the humanities reflect a specifically American or at least Western, modern, and secular version of human being and human flourishing, and that the entire concept might be a mere provincial prejudice.[2]

The humanities might be suspect as an imperialist extrapolation, apparently assuming that that which is familiar in one's own context would also be typical elsewhere. Despite such concerns, I am convinced that the ideals of scholarship involved do have global significance. Only an ambition that is universal allows our knowledge and understanding to be challenged for not doing enough justice to the diversity of human experiences and perspectives we encounter. Harpham's change of mind, as an example of self-reflective sensitivity to diversity due to context, past and present, is typical for the humanities.

To characterize the humanities, I offer the following tentative definition:

> Humanities are academic disciplines in which humans seek understanding of human self-understandings and self-expressions, and of the ways in which people thereby construct and experience the world they live in.

This definition presents the humanities as a second-order activity. The basis is, of course, that as humans we express ourselves. A few of us write novels or poetry, or create art that expresses feelings of the artist or evokes a response in the observer. Behind all those human expressions we assume an inner world; humans have intentions when they act. So, too, when experiencing people, we encounter the cultural world in which they live. The world has not merely an impact on them, but all humans are subjects experiencing the world. Acting and

2 Geoffrey Galt Harpham, *The Humanities and the Dream of America* (University of Chicago Press, 2011), p. 8.

perceiving, creating and reading: such activities and experiences are typically human. This is the diverse realm of first-order activities which the humanities study.

In the humanities, we reflect upon human expressions. In literary studies we study texts humans have written; in art history other forms of expression; in cultural analysis the dynamics of individuals, groups, and societies; in linguistics and communication studies verbal and nonverbal communication. As the humanities study human expressions, it is a second-order activity. There must be humans before there can be humanities.

The humanities even include third-order projects. Historians can study the history of ways of writing history. Philosophers can seek to understand the humanities, that is, seek understanding of the understanding of human self-understandings and self-expressions. That is what I hope to do here; one might consider these pages a contribution to a philosophy of the humanities.

A definition of the humanities that also stresses human agency, is one given by Stefan Collini in his *What Are Universities For?* He writes,

> the label "humanities" is now taken to embrace that collection of disciplines which attempt to understand, across barriers of time and culture, the actions and creations of other human beings considered as bearers of meaning, where the emphasis tends to fall on matters to do with individual and cultural distinctiveness and not on matters which are primarily susceptible to characterization in purely statistical or biological terms.[3]

In the humanities we approach other human beings "as bearers of meaning." Their actions and creations are not random events, but are supposed to have meaning to them. If one encounters an object from a time long past, say a clay tablet with cuneiform inscriptions, experts try to decipher the text – perhaps a contract, a letter, or a fragment of the Gilgamesh epos. The scholar assumes that the scratches on the clay tablet convey something that was meaningful to those who made them, whether for practical purposes as an inventory of goods delivered or a record of promises made, or expressive of their identity

3 Collini, *What Are Universities For?*, p. 64.

as a record of their conquests or their beliefs about an afterlife. They were subjects too, experiencing their world, articulating their identity, and acting within their context.

However, the formulation by Collini focuses on "other human beings," whereas the humanities may be about ourselves as well. Self-understanding is central to the rationale for the humanities articulated by Geoffrey Galt Harpham:[4]

> *The scholarly study of documents and artifacts produced by human beings in the past enables us to see the world from different points of view so that we may better understand ourselves.*

I do not see why we should restrict ourselves to documents "from the past," though a historical orientation characterizes much scholarship in the humanities, nor study in particular "documents," even though "documents and artifacts" may be taken to include nonliteral features such as the layout of a city or the rituals of a community. But the confrontation with a plurality of "other points of view" makes the humanities an engaging area of scholarly study.

PURSUING KNOWLEDGE

The humanities provide knowledge, just as do other sciences. Whereas the definition given above started with the human as a subject, as someone who seeks understanding of the world, including understanding of the acts of other humans, one might also begin with the world as the object of study. Such an approach would be more typical of the natural sciences, but such an "objective" intention, providing knowledge of the world, is there also within the humanities. In order to clarify the character of the humanities as scholarly disciplines, we will begin with similarities and dissimilarities with the natural sciences.

They are similar in studying what is "out there," *particulars*. Our cultural world has an enormous variety of languages, histories, artistic expressions, and much else, each worthy of careful study. So, too, has biology when it studies micro-organisms, plants, and animals in various ecosystems. So too in chemistry, as experiments are about

4 Harpham, *The Humanities and the Dream of America*, p. 23 (italics in original).

particular substances interacting with each other. The study of particulars deserves priority; one cannot study linguistics without studying one or more languages.

Humanities provide us with knowledge of particulars in relation to the contexts in which they function. Religious, artistic, and cultural traditions; ritual practices and literatures; living conditions of families; and much else can be studied in detail and in depth, so that we may come to know a specific practice in its historical development and context. As an analogy from the natural sciences, one might think of biology. In botany and zoology, one studies plants and animals, to uncover their particular constitution, behavior, and development, relative to the ecological setting they are involved in. Or one might think of astronomy, where astrophysicists study galaxies, stars, and, today, even exoplanets, planetary systems around other stars, to uncover the variety that turns out to be there, and discover the conditions under which particular systems have formed and continue to exist. In the humanities, comparative research on particulars is important too, as it allows to discern patterns, or their absence, and thus helps us see what is specific to a particular human practice.

The level of analysis, and thus the units under consideration, may differ from one research project to another. It may be a history of the Roman Empire or of the Industrial Revolution in Europe, but it may also be a study of one burial site, a single poem, or even the grammatical functions of one word. The more focus, the greater the depth that can be achieved. As units of analysis, one may think of cultural groups that are fairly homogeneous, relative to their wider environment, say when studying migrant minorities in a multicultural society. But though focusing on the plurality of groups may be useful as an approximation, diversity at the individual level is always even greater. Many influences come together in an individual life; persons may have multiple identities. So, too, for works of art, historical developments, and other human phenomena: As expressions of human inventiveness, as different from all others, they are unique. In their "singularity," human expressions – in literature, art, and otherwise – are meaningful, and, hence, relevant for research.[5]

5 Derek Attridge, *The Singularity of Literature* (London: Routledge, 2004).

Languages change, and so do religions, cultural traditions, styles in art and literature, and much else. They may change due to migration, by adaptation to new circumstances, and by appropriation of elements from others. They may also change due to the fact that they are studied. The knowledge outsiders develop may have an impact on the social and cultural reality that is studied. In this respect, the situation in the humanities differs from research in astrophysics; our knowledge of other planetary systems does not change those. In biology, the human presence does change ecosystems, but ecosystems are not directly influenced by the ideas of biologists, but by our practices, whether those of tourists or of conservationists.

Let me illustrate the influence of the humanities on the human practice studied with an example about Zoroastrianism, a religious tradition that arose in Persia centuries "Before the Common Era," BCE, according to the Western calendar. Within this tradition, rituals play a major role, supported by their collection of sacred literature, the Avesta. One part of this text, the Yashna, is the text of the daily high ritual. In the nineteenth century, a German scholar of Sanskrit, Martin Haug, argued on the basis of linguistic analysis that a tiny portion of the Yashna, five poems called the Gathas, were in a more archaic dialect than the rest of the Avesta, and hence, he concluded, these were older. Zoroastrians might have responded with indifference, "so what?" Or they could have rejected the scholarly conclusion, as at odds with the way they understood their own tradition. Something else happened; the scholarly discovery was appropriated by the Parsis, the Zoroastrians of the Indian subcontinent. Within Zoroastrianism, the Gathas now have become more important than other texts in the Avesta.[6]

In this case, the scholar not only studied a tradition; through his work he redefined it. The language of a tradition may change as well, as scholarly, analytical concepts, and insights may become actor concepts and thereby more indirectly reshape the self-understanding of

6 Albert F. De Jong, "Historians of Religion as Agents of Religious Change," in Willem B. Drees and Pieter Sjoerd van Koningsveld (eds.), *The Study of Religion and the Training of Muslim Clergy in Europe* (Leiden University Press, 2007), 195–218, p. 206f.

the believers. Thus, in studying cultural traditions, one should be alert to the possibility that these have been influenced by earlier scholarship.

An interest of the scholar is to gather knowledge about others, in their linguistic, historical, and cultural diversity. In the effort to learn about humans in their diversity, the scholar should not be judgmental, but rather be methodologically agnostic. The scholarly interest lies in what words or practices mean (or meant) to the humans studied. The question is not whether the scholar shares those beliefs or values. The intention is to understand them. How do they see their world? How do they see their history, and how do they relate to their past? How do they use their language? What would they consider art?

When we ask what was meaningful to them, we treat them as persons, as subjects. Thus, though there is a major similarity with the natural sciences, in seeking to envisage the diversity of life forms and of cultural practices, there is a difference in the nature of the object. The objects of the humanities are themselves also subjects; they are humans using language to communicate, engaging in practices meaningful to them.

Underlying similarities and mechanisms are of great interest to biologists studying the multitude of life forms. So, too, for scholars in the humanities. Though there are many different human languages and cultures, there are similarities between human experiences and practices at different times and places. At least, such is the case according to Rens Bod in his book *A New History of the Humanities: The Search for Principles and Patterns from Antiquity to the Present.* The humanities even preceded the natural sciences by developing systematic approaches and discovering patterns in human languages, literatures and other texts, music, and other art forms, as described in grammar, musical theory, logic, art theory, and many other disciplines. In philology, early modern humanists such as Erasmus have discovered a lot about types of unintentional mistakes and intentional changes that slip into texts when copied. Lessons learned about the way to construct the history of a text from tiny copying errors, served well when humans started to construct biological history from mutations in DNA. Computer programming owes much to linguistics, with its insights about recursive rules. Bod thus presents the humanities as sciences, searching for patterns, "general laws" based on sophisticated observations and occasional experiments.

In seeking to uncover patterns, the emphasis is on what humans do, rather than on what the texts, objects, and practices mean to the people involved. Bod considers briefly whether there has not been a major shift in the nineteenth century, with the emergence of a distinction between the natural sciences, with the interest in explanations in terms of natural laws (*erklären*), and the humanities, focusing on unique events, to be understood as meaningful to humans (*verstehen*). However, Bod argues that the main change in the nineteenth century was institutional, separating faculties of natural sciences and of humanities in the universities, rather than substantial, as research in both domains continued to look for patterns.

Bod judges that in more recent times, in the second half of the twentieth century, a significant split arose *within* the humanities, a split between those who search for patterns, for instance via computational analysis, and, in contrast, those who emphasize the unique character of events, an orientation typical of postmodern movements. The search for patterns is dominant in linguistics, whereas a pattern-rejecting orientation is more common in literary studies, musicology, and art history. Bod finds precursors to this pattern-rejecting tradition in the Hellenistic world of the third century BCE. Whereas in Alexandria, arguments based on regularity-oriented analogies between forms of words were used, he finds that in Pergamon, Chrysippus and others were focusing primarily on differences and exceptions. Their method was less systematic.

> Nevertheless, the anomalistic approach produced a number of extraordinarily original works. The anomalists – unlike the analogists, whose work was mostly formal – produced erudite commentaries. For example, Demetrius of Scepsis wrote a series of thirty books about the Trojan forces, which were addressed in fewer than sixty-two lines in the entire *Iliad*. Every point of view was dissected by the author, using a vast quantity of literature, local and oral traditions, history, mythology, geography, poetry, and observations by travelers – in other words, he called upon the entirety of classical knowledge to contribute to the interpretation of the text. This detailed and particularistic approach was developed in Pergamon and since then has never disappeared from the humanities. We will come across

> anominalists in many different guises. It survived both the Middle Ages and the early modern age, was regenerated in nineteenth-century hermeneutics, and reached a provisional pinnacle in twentieth-century poststructuralism.[7]

They prefer to focus on the author's intentions and the pragmatic ways in which texts are used, rather than on general patterns. Bod remains reserved about the rule-rejecting approach: "The erudite, detailed exegeses from Pergamon are perhaps the finest that the classical humanities generated. But is it scholarship or literary art? Whatever the case may be, the results of the anomalists cannot be verified empirically, let alone replicated. But then again, that was far from their intention."[8]

With respect to the disciplinary landscape in our time, Bod articulates similar reservations about cultural studies. They have no clear method, though, nonetheless, they may uncover trends and patterns not discerned before. "For example, new relationships between power and knowledge have surfaced, and persistent myths about the accessibility of the digital world and the oneness of national identity have been negated. This 'boundless diversity of present-day culture' is precisely what cultural studies is aiming at. As a hybrid discipline, however, it lacks a clear basis that guarantees any controllability."[9]

Bod's preference is clearly on the side of well-structured, methodical analysis. He expects that the humanities will benefit from cognitive approaches, importing knowledge from psychology, and from digital approaches that provide new tools to analyze texts and other data, and hence will allow us to ask new questions. The rise of new disciplines such as media studies and cultural studies, drawing on methods from various fields, is also productive, though he warns for the danger "lurking in the uncritical combination of different scholarly fields."[10] It seems to me, that someone speaking on behalf of cultural studies, broadly conceived, might raise the same concern about the appropriation of methods from psychology and computer sciences, as these

7 Rens Bod, *A New History of the Humanities: The Search for Patterns and Principles from Antiquity to the Present* (Oxford University Press, 2013), p. 33

8 Bod, *A New History of the Humanities*, p. 35

9 Bod, *A New History of the Humanities*, p. 342.

10 Bod, *A New History of the Humanities*, p. 362.

may make us focus on some questions at the expense of questions inspired by other perspectives.

Bod's emphasis in his *New History of the Humanities* is on pattern seeking approaches, which he finds again and again at various places and times in different research areas. But at the end of his book he speaks in favor of diversity within the humanities.

> I started this book with a quest for pattern-seeking activities in the humanities, but towards the end it emerges that the pattern-rejecting tradition is at least as fascinating. We would be better advised not to just put up with the versatility of the humanities, but to embrace it.[11]

Even this strong advocate of humanities as pattern-seeking, similar to the sciences, thus expects a positive contribution from an orientation that emphasizes uniqueness over regularities and similarities.

In the search for patterns, and perhaps even laws, and in the effort to understand the diversity of particulars, the humanities may be comparable to the natural sciences, especially to those that have a temporal and thus "a historical" dimension, such as astronomy and biology. Scientists are studying individual phenomena and processes, say galaxies, plants, or bacteria, and their behavior, and they seek to grasp the underling mechanisms that gave rise to this diversity. So, too, do scholars in the humanities. But we ourselves are humans. We are not just studying others; we engage with them, as fellow humans; we act, as humans do. As the study of humans, the humanities may be compared to the social sciences – and there, too, we encounter similarities and differences.

AGENTS AND ACTORS

In *The Philosophy of Social Science: An Introduction*, Martin Hollis distinguishes between humans as agents and as actors. As he uses these terms, one might consider *agents* all entities that change their environment. Even the weather is an agent. Agents are causally effective; the wind may push a boat forward gently. Blowing angrily, the storm may make trees topple. "Gently" and "angrily" are nice metaphors. However, animism is not a live option for us. The wind does not

11 Bod, *A New History of the Humanities*, p. 363.

intend anything by making a tree fall; it just blows. Neither "gently" nor "angrily" is applicable, except for the way the wind is experienced by humans. We might explain why the wind blows by offering a causal explanation in terms of areas with high pressure and low pressure; we would not refer to its intentions or its mood. Similarly, one may have an economic model for the most efficient, "rational" choices consumers will make to satisfy their preferences. Such a model may draw on game theory. In such a way, the analysis of human behavior abstracts from their moods, principles, and reasons.

But humans are not merely agents, whose behavior may be modelled. Humans are also *actors*, who act for a reason, who have intentions. Whereas with the explanatory approach, rules may be descriptive, to be discovered as statistical patterns in observations, for human actors rules can be prescriptive, normative, indicating how one should act. At least how, according to the people involved, one should act, drawing on their values and ideals. When treating humans as actors, we recognize their inner lives, the motives that may drive them, the meaning they may attach to certain practices, and the interpretations they give to the world. With the distinction between considering humans as agents and as actors, Hollis distinguished between two approaches to human behavior, characterized by the words *explanation* and *understanding*.

This distinction emerged in the nineteenth century as a way to understand the humanities, or in the scholarly German of the period, the *Geisteswissenschaften*, well before the social sciences in their modern form emerged. Hollis associates "explaining" with a naturalistic approach, seeking to explain and predict what happens by drawing on models that include various causal factors. In contrast, "understanding" is associated with an interpretative approach. "Its central proposition is that the social world must be understood from within, rather than explained from without. Instead of seeking the causes of behavior, we are to seek the meaning of action. Actions derive their meaning from the shared ideas and rules of social life and are performed by actors who mean something by them."[12] Hollis considers

12 Martin Hollis, *The Philosophy of Social Science: An Introduction* (Cambridge University Press, 1994), pp. 16–17; similarly, Martin Hollis, *Reason in Action: Essays in the Philosophy of Social Science* (Cambridge University Press, 1996).

this a rival tradition within the social sciences; it may be more typical of cultural anthropology than of economics. He does not discuss the humanities as such, but one might use these distinctions to make clear that in the humanities, the emphasis is on humans as actors, who have an inner life, whereas in the social sciences the explanatory orientation with its emphasis on models, statistics, and aspirations of objectivity, tends to take the first place.

In the humanities we also have a quest for explanatory models. This is more clearly the case when we consider not the individual level but larger collectives. In the context of explanatory approaches, Hollis stresses that individual agents operate in the context of larger wholes, structures, or systems; to a large extent, their behavior is determined by the context in which they operate. So too, of course, when we speak: if we want to be understood, we draw upon the language that is available to us, follow its grammatical rules and operate with the words, whose meanings may be looked up in dictionaries. But we use the available vocabulary and grammatical rules to express our intentions or feelings; what we *do* with language goes beyond the linguistic system. We also do not even have to follow its regularities, as we may use language in creative ways. The rules of a language are not causes that determine how we must speak; they are tools that we affirm or revise, to express ourselves.

Approaching humans as *actors*, to whom the world means something, who have intentions, who act for reasons, aligns well with common sense, with our personal interactions in life, outside the scholarly world. In the humanities we seek to understand others, our fellow humans. Scholarship in the humanities aspires to be a quest to understand the self-understanding of another person or community, to understand how they experience the world, and to learn from the others I encounter, perhaps even to engage in a dialogue with others. In the way we speak about such engagement, there is in grammar the second person, the moment I address you and you speak to me. We encounter others, and engage each other. Does a message come across as intended? Do I understand you correctly?

A technical term for such issues of interpretative understanding, and potential misunderstanding, is *hermeneutics*. Not only do we seek knowledge about others in their specificity, and perhaps strangeness.

Those others are fellow humans, and we might therefore learn from them something relevant to ourselves as well. Or, at least, we owe it to them as humans to try to understand their motives, the way the world appears to them. That we owe it to them is a moral conviction, reflecting the moral weight of speaking of humanity. How might we come to see the world if we came to share their perspective?

Such work in the humanities might develop from research that focuses on specific ideas and particular practices, combined with some sense of general patterns that helps to make it intelligible how their view reflects their place and time, and how it might be appropriated in other circumstances such as mine. It involves scholarly knowledge, but moves in a different direction than one would do in a quest for patterns. The movement is not toward a phonetic script or some other tool that abstracts from the particular, and thereby would allow for comparative or historical, diachronic analysis. However, neither does a scholarly effort to understand someone else imply that one should replace analysis by empathy, that understanding necessarily involves agreement.

The effort to understand the ideas and actions of others and consider their potential relevance for me, goes well beyond the academic distance considered typical of the natural sciences. It also goes beyond the "objective" aspirations, in the description and analysis of particulars and the search for general patterns, described above. Nevertheless, it should be a serious, scholarly effort. There is something to be discovered, something truthful and interesting about the meaning the world has to someone else. In the next chapter we will begin our exploration of the humanities by developing further this dimension of the humanities, as an effort to get to know fellow humans.

We humans care about ourselves. Who am I? What is troubling me? What can I believe? What is meaningful to someone else, may have meaning for me. Insights about others, may help us understand ourselves. Reflexivity in the humanities brings us to a fourth type of knowledge. Whereas the search for knowledge about particulars and patterns is fairly similar to research in the natural sciences, the hermeneutical focus considered above, and this self-reflexive move are specific to the humanities.

We may reflect on reasoning: How should I argue? What are sound arguments? What are the criteria? Similarly, about moral and aesthetic judgements: What should I do? What are the criteria for sound moral deliberation and for aesthetic appreciation? What is the status of moral claims? There are methodological and meta-ethical questions, about the conditions for life, knowledge, and action. As we live our lives, we implicitly understand our own existence and obligations, we have a "practical self-understanding."

To reflect upon our self-understanding, our assumptions, and biases, our identity, is typical of philosophy. But it also involves the way we relate to the historical legacies that shape us and our context. This includes cultural and national legacies, for most of Europe varieties of the Christian tradition, humanism, Enlightenment, and modernity; elsewhere, other legacies might be more relevant. The study of the religious beliefs and practices of others is part of the humanities, but as a reflection upon one's identity and convictions in relation to traditional resources, systematic theology and humanistic philosophy can be considered part of the humanities too. The humanities as self-understanding, as reflection upon our judgements and our identities, will be central to the third chapter.

After having considered the humanities as the effort to understand others and ourselves, we will turn in the fourth chapter to the humanities as responsible scholarship. Together, these three chapters develop my view of the humanities as a scholarly domain, as an answer to the question of *Part I What Are the Humanities?* The chapters in the second part of the book will consider the humanities beyond the academic context.

WHO NEEDS THE HUMANITIES?

Texts, whether literature, holy books, or laws, are the material for scholarly interpretative analysis. However, they also form the fabric of our social life. Not only scholars are engaged in interpretation, but so, too, are lawyers, religious leaders, and many others. To what extent is their work guided by the same standards as scholarly interpretation in the humanities? We will consider the role of professional interpretation, in particular in legal and religious contexts, in Chapter 5.

Humanities are understood here as a second-order activity, by humans, about humans. To understand the humanities better, in the sixth chapter we will reflect upon "human nature," upon the animal that is central to the humanities.

The humanities operate in today's world. Why would it be relevant to invest some of our time and resources in the humanities? In the final chapter, we will argue for the relevance of the humanities, on the basis of the understanding of the humanities developed in the preceding chapters. As a preview, let us consider three different approaches, argued for in recent years.

A hermeneutical motive, and, to some extent, also a self-reflective one, is central to Martha Nussbaum's *Not for Profit: Why Democracy Needs the Humanities.*[13] She emphasizes the development of empathy, of appreciating the perspectives of others, the ability to spot abuse of language and of power, and the ability to engage in civil disagreement and hence political discourse.

The emphasis on knowledge that aspires to be as objective as feasible, especially knowledge of patterns, is central to *A New History of the Humanities: The Search for Principles and Patterns from Antiquity to the Present* by Rens Bod. Fundamental research, also in the humanities, may become useful because it provides insight in fundamental patterns. The focus should be on knowledge itself, not on its application, as fundamental knowledge in the long run delivers the best applications.

In *The Value of the Humanities*, literary scholar Helen Small offers a more pluralistic view of the humanities. Smart has reservations about an overstatement of the critical public role, but neither does she share the exclusive emphasis on science-like knowledge. Small holds that "the humanities matter for their own sake."[14] I agree with Helen Small that the humanities matter intrinsically, for their own sake. That is why my argument for the relevance of the humanities needs to start with a reflection on the character of the humanities. Which brings us back to the main ambition of this book, understanding the humanities, beginning in the next chapter, on the claim that in the humanities we seek to understand fellow humans.

13 Martha Nussbaum, *Not for Profit: Why Society Needs the Humanities* (Princeton University Press, 2010).

14 Helen Small, *The Value of the Humanities* (Oxford University Press, 2013), p. 6.

2

Understanding Others

We humans are social beings. We live with others. We need each other. It takes a village to raise a child, as an African saying has it. The need for partners, colleagues, and friends applies to almost anything else as well. Also, as more and more people live in cities, while home, work, and recreation have become distinct spheres of life, the circle of others we interact with has expanded enormously. We have even come to speak of the "global village," though that suggests too much familiarity.

To understand others when they speak to us, directly or through their writings and their nonverbal messages, their actions, and their art, we need to learn their language and to know their context, their place. Not only do we seek knowledge about others, whether familiar or strange; we also would like to understand how they see themselves. By words and actions they speak to their contemporaries, but across distances in space and time we might meet them too. Even if we do not expect to learn from them something that could be relevant to us, we owe it to them as fellow humans to attempt to understand the way the world appears to them.

To say that "we owe it to them" rests on a moral conviction, one that I include in the meaning of humanity and of humanities. In Harper Lee's *To Kill a Mocking Bird*, a novel that explores racism in the southern United States in the early twentieth century, a father tells his daughter, "First of all, if you can learn a simple trick, Scout, you'll get along a lot better with all kinds of folk. You never really understand a person until you consider things from his point of view – until you climb into his skin and walk around in it."[1] To live with others as neighbors in the global village we need to be able to consider things from their point of view.

When we meet others, we assume that the other is a subject, an actor, someone to whom the world is meaningful, someone who uses language to express something. There is something to be discovered – the meaning the world has to those fellow humans, their history and culture. But the scholars need not agree with the people they encounter and study. Also, the people studied may be offended by the way the scholar describes and understands their history. We will consider examples of tension between scholars and those studied later in this chapter. Engaging others is not necessarily all peace and harmony. Before discussing efforts to understand others and the tensions this may give rise to, the core of this chapter, we will consider the basic tools involved, the study of *languages* and *contexts.*

HUMAN TOOLS: LANGUAGES

There are thousands of different languages. There are languages currently spoken and languages of a distant past. Some languages were written with spikes in clay tablets, in hieroglyphs, and other scripts that are unfamiliar to me. There are languages from native communities in Africa and South America; from China, Korea, and Japan; and from countries closer to my Dutch home, such as English, French, and German. The humanities are not short on languages to study.

There are various questions about languages one might ask. What is their internal structure or their grammar? Does each language distinguish verbs and nouns? How are experiences and ideas shaped by language? Does it make a difference whether a message is conveyed in sound, in script, through gestures, or coded in some other way? How is the brain generating and processing language? How do languages change over time? How are our languages changed by new technologies, from writing to printing, and now the Internet and smartphone? Are there multiple linguistic families, such as the Indo-European one, or do all languages spring from a single source in human evolution? To

1 Harper Lee, *To Kill a Mockingbird* (Philadelphia: Lippincott, 1960), p. 32.

what extent is language determined by our biology, and to what extent is it better understood in social, historical, and cultural terms? Linguistics, the study of language and languages, is a vast domain of knowledge within the humanities. Linguists address such questions in research. They have well-grounded answers to various questions and theoretical insights about language and the way humans, with our biological and cognitive capacities, produce language.

Within that domain, the study of what people *do* with language might be called pragmatics. The meaning of an utterance is conveyed by words, but it also depends on prosody, the way it is spoken – with emphasis or with silences, the way a speaker uses stress and tone. It also depends on the context. By focusing on communication, including nonverbal communication, one focuses on humans as actors, as speakers of language. Language use also involves what people say and write, the literature and the tweets in which they express ideas and emotions.

Learning a language opens the door to learning about the way humans express themselves, interact with each other, and experience the social, cultural, and material world. Understanding what is said in a language requires far more than merely learning the meaning of words and memorizing the dictionary. To understand a joke or recognize an allusion, one needs to be attentive to the way words are used and the context that is assumed. Such a broader ability to use a language opens up the literature of a people, their culture, and their world. Language may also be used ironically, to evoke something else, or to lie, to mislead about intentions, or to hide one's ideas. Discerning what people convey depends on understanding language as used at a particular time and place.

There are vastly more languages than any individual can handle. Hence, to make cross-cultural understanding possible, for trade or war, for scholarship and among friends, we need interpreters and translators. Alternatively, we need to have a shared language, a *lingua franca*, like Latin once served as the scholarly language in Europe. In the future, new technologies might make interpreters unnecessary, but at the moment, automatic translations still feel shallow.

Reliance on translations or on a shared language has disadvantages. Languages do not match. For one word in the original, there might be three or more ways to express the same idea in the other language. Alternatively, there might be none that expresses precisely the same idea, but two or three express more or less the same idea, depending on the context. Nuances and associations may be lost and ambiguities introduced. Even within a single language, the same word may have different meanings, dependent upon the dialect — for the Flemish, "middag" refers to the two hours between noon and 2:00 PM, whereas for the Dutch the same word refers to the whole afternoon, from 12:00 PM until 6:00 PM.

Learning more than only one's mother tongue enriches one's sensibility to the complexity of understanding, within one's own linguistic environment but even more across cultures and historical periods. However, one's time is limited, while the universe of languages is almost inexhaustible. Depending on abilities, it may be feasible to acquire competence in a few languages but never in all.

Nonetheless, we need ways to understand each other, even though we have different mother tongues. As long as automatic translation is not good enough, using a shared second language is the more efficient approach. Assume we have to take a mere 50 languages into consideration. If we were to work with translators who could translate from A to B and also from B to A, we would need well over 1,000 such translators (50 × 49, for the source and target languages, divided by 2). If we worked with one mediating language such as Latin, we could do with just fifty, from each of these languages into Latin and vice versa. Also, if all people involved were sufficiently competent in the same second language, we could even do without translators.

Thus, given the multitude of languages in our pluralist world, we would be served well if we were to have a shared second language. Esperanto, a language intentionally created in the late nineteenth century as a neutral vehicle, failed, as it lacked political clout. De facto, the mediating language in the world today has become English, which is why I write this book in English – not just for Britons, Americans, and Australians but for readers from many different linguistic backgrounds. That English has acquired such a global role is due to accidental historical developments; its position reflects political dominance. Latin was prominent due to the Roman Empire and thereafter the dominance of the Catholic Church in large parts of Europe. English rose in standing due to the British colonial empire and subsequently global American dominance, politically but also culturally; think of Hollywood.

English need not be the best tool for the purpose. It has peculiar features, to some extent due to a shift in the pronunciation of vowels some 500 years ago, leading to a substantial mismatch between spoken and written English. Words that look the same, such as "to go" and "to do," are pronounced rather differently, thereby easily confusing non-native speakers. By being used by many non-native speakers, the language itself is affected. I learned of "Euro English" as a designation for varieties of English as used in Europe. Also, the availability of English affects other languages; words migrate and are appropriated. In various contexts, including advertisements and communication on Twitter, we see combinations of English and the local language – hybridization. The study of such linguistic developments, and the way they reflect social dynamics, is an interesting branch of sociolinguistics, which also can be seen as a form of cultural studies.

English has its home base in the UK and the USA, but also in Canada, Ireland, and other countries. Native speakers have an advantage, though this also can be a disadvantage: Those who have no familiarity with at least one other language may find it more difficult to understand people with other linguistic backgrounds.

With English comes particular content. Shared references are drawn most often from cultural resources associated with English and hence from the plays written by William Shakespeare (England, sixteenth century) rather than from those by Henrik Ibsen (Norway, nineteenth century), let alone from a non-Western author. Using English as a single common language has its risks. One should be alert to inequalities and the cultural bias that might come with it. But using English as a shared second language does allow for cross-cultural communication and collaboration in our globalizing world.

CONTEXTS: PLACES AND SPACES

Acquiring knowledge about others involves much more than just learning their language. One also needs to know their situation, the context within which they live. In cultural studies, some colleagues speak of "spaces"; in area studies I came across the term "places," where "place" stands not only for a geographical location but also for culture and politics, for the worlds people live in, and continuously modify by living in it. Here, I will draw my examples from some of the approaches called area studies.[2] Such research might also go by region-specific names such as Asia studies or, even more specific, China studies. The more specific the label, the more a place, with its history and culture, is studied in depth. A more general label, in contrast, invites one to analyze the interactions between various regions and to engage in comparative work, across specific places.

Historically, research on specific countries, regions, or linguistic groups often has been to the service of colonial and imperial dominance. Global issues such as the Cold War and more recent concerns about terrorism and migration have shaped Western research on non-Western cultures and countries. Note that, with this paragraph, I shifted from a general description of area studies as the study of various cultures and countries to the study of *non-Western* cultures and countries. Area studies tends to be the study of others, and some cultures appear to be more other than others. Occasionally, one may also have at a European university a program for North America studies or one on European studies, but these tend to be more specific on policy issues and international relations than would be a department for China studies, which covers the study of language, literature, history, culture, art, philosophy, and religion in China. For the West, some of those other aspects are categorized as separate disciplines, such as cultural studies, philosophy, and history.

Even when area studies no longer serve colonial dominance, the Western engagement with the languages, art, culture, philosophy, and religion of people in a non-Western region might be looked upon with ambivalence. How should we relate to that which belongs to others, that which arose in a different cultural context? Studying others, the non-West, is also a postcolonial confrontation with Western culture, as we study its impact on other places and our biases and interests in understanding and appropriating the lives of others.[3]

2 Maghiel Van Crevel, "China Awareness, Area Studies, High School Chinese: Here to Stay, and Looking Forward," in W. L. Idema (ed.), *Chinese Studies in the Netherlands: Past, Present and Future* (Leiden: Brill, 2014), 263–273.

3 Arjun Appadurai, *Modernity at Large: Cultural Dimensions of Globalization* (Minneapolis: University of Minnesota Press, 1996); Colin Campbell, *The*

As a historical case study of some of the complexities involved, one might consider the book series *Sacred Books of the East,* published by Oxford University Press between 1879 and 1910. The series was the initiative of Friedrich Max Müller (1823–1900), professor of comparative linguistics at Oxford University. With the growing awareness that there was a single linguistic family that stretched from India to Europe, the Indo-European languages, there was in the West an increased interest in texts in Sanskrit and other languages from India, and in "the East" more generally speaking. The fifty-volume series offered English translations of religious books and manuscripts, mostly from British colonial territories such as India. It was a large-scale project in the humanities, comparable to big science in our time. Müller considered eight religious traditions of particular importance due to the books they had, namely – referring to them by key persons, as one does for Christianity – from India and Persia, Brahmanism [Hinduism], Buddhism, and Zoroastrianism; from the Middle East, Mosaism [Judaism], Christianity, and Mohammedanism [Islam]; and from China, Confucianism and Daoism. According to Müller, the book series shows that "we are not the only people who have a Bible"; he spoke of "Forgotten Bibles."[4] His original proposal had included the Hebrew Bible and the New Testament, in a series to be titled Sacred Books of Mankind, but including Christianity on equal footing alongside other religions met with too much resistance in England in his time.

Despite the exclusion of the sources of Christianity, the series was not merely a scholarly collection; it was also intended to serve as a religious resource for Europeans. In 1874, in an opening address as president of the Aryan section of the International Congress of Orientalists, Müller said,

> We know now that in language, and in all that is implied by language, India and Europe are one. . . . We say no longer vaguely

Easternization of the West: A Thematic Account of Cultural Change in the Modern Era (Boulder, CO: Paradigm Publishers, 2007).

4 Arie L. Molendijk, *Friedrich Max Müller and the Sacred Books of the East* (Oxford University Press, 2016), p. 7; Friedrich Max Müller, "Forgotten Bibles," in: *Last Essays, Second Series: Essays on the Science of Religion* (London: Longmans, Green and Co., 1901), 1–35, p. 33.

> *Ex Oriente Lux* [Light from the East], but we know that all the most vital elements of our knowledge and civilisation ... come to us from the East. ... The East is ours, we are its heirs, and claim by right our share in its inheritance.[5]

Such an appropriation might not be so well received in our time, but his Orientalism showed admiration and sympathy for "the East." The series of books was received well by those who with greater right could claim to be heirs to these books. The series and the preceding discovery of a shared linguistic background contributed to the self-esteem of people in India and supported Hindus in their view of India as "the cradle of higher civilization *tout court*," as Arie Molendijk points out in his biography of this book series.[6]

In his *Introduction to the Science of Religion*, Müller expressed his conviction that the study of other religions would be beneficial for Christianity as well.

> That study, I feel convinced, if carried on in a bold, but scholar-like, careful, and reverent spirit, will remove many doubts and difficulties which are due entirely to the narrowness of our religious horizon; it will enlarge our sympathies, it will raise our thoughts above the small controversies of the day, and at no distant future evoke in the very heart of Christianity a fresh spirit, and a new life.[7]

He treats Christianity as the highest form of religion. His focus is ethical and experiential rather than doctrinal and confessional. The emphasis on texts is both an academic and a Protestant one, while the religious focus is liberal rather than orthodox, as he gives precedence to morality and spirituality over dogma. His was clearly a religiously engaged reception of religious plurality, within a frame that treated his own culture as the most advanced one.

5 Friedrich Max Müller, "Opening Address, Delivered by the President of the Aryan Section at the International Congress of Orientalists, Held in London, September 14–21, 1874," in *Chips from a German Workshop, Volume IV: Essays Chiefly on the Science of Language* (New York: Charles Scribner's Sons, 1895), 317–358, pp. 324–326.

6 Molendijk, *Friedrich Max Müller and the Sacred Books of the East*, p. 2.

7 Friedrich Max Müller, *Introduction to the Science of Religion* (London: Longmans, Green, and Co., 1873), p. ix.

In area studies, scholars are reserved about appropriation, about playing down differences and about placing others in an evolutionary scheme that considers "us" the more civilized ones. An outspoken article concerned about appropriation was titled "Lead Us Not into Translation," treating translation as the temptation to make the other fit into our categories. Rather, we should read their stories "as a tale of otherness, difference, and dissent that lets us call into question the epistemic violence of scientific incorporation."[8]

Let me illustrate the need for sensitivity to differences with a contemporary case about Buddhism and its reception in the West as a science-friendly philosophy. In this case, appropriation is not so much the scholar's contribution, as it was with Müller, but it characterizes the cultural reception of Buddhism in the West and its transformation into something new, Western Buddhism. The Fourteenth Dalai Lama is a global ambassador for Buddhism, arguing for a positive relation with modern science. He is the author of *The Universe in a Single Atom: The Convergence of Science and Spirituality*, and, assisted by interpreters, engages scientists in the Mind and Life conferences.[9] His engagement with science and scientists makes Buddhism attractive in the West. At the same time, he also makes science acceptable to the Tibetan community. The Dalai Lama engages younger monks in those meetings and initiated a separate program, Science for Monks.

From Donald S. Lopez, a scholar of Buddhism, I learned that science-friendly spiritual and philosophical Buddhism is not representative of historical Buddhism as it developed in Asia.[10] As a historian, he points to substantial diversity within Buddhism. In the nineteenth century, Western scholars became most familiar with the Buddhism of Sri Lanka and South-East Asia, Theravada Buddhism, and the Pali canon; among the Western partners, Spiritism and Theosophy were prominent. After World War II, Zen Buddhism became *en vogue*. In recent decades, Tibetan Buddhism, represented by the Dalai Lama,

8 Michael Robert Dutton, "Lead Us Not into Translation: Notes toward a Theoretical Foundation for Asian Studies." *Nepantia: Views from the South* 3 (2002), 495–537, p. 527.

9 The Dalai Lama, *The Universe in a Single Atom: The Convergence of Science and Spirituality* (New York: Morgan Road Books, 2005).

10 Donald S. Lopez, *Buddhism and Science: A Guide for the Perplexed* (University of Chicago Press, 2008).

became the archetypical Buddhism. The Dalai Lama's engagement with science might be seen as functional in a missionary competition between Tibetan Buddhism, Zen Buddhism, and Theravada Buddhism, as each seeks to shape Western Buddhism.

Tibetan Buddhism is not monolithic either. There are four major schools, among them the Gelug to which the Dalai Lama belongs. Indicative of competition within Tibetan Buddhism is the observation by Donald Lopez that the Dalai Lama occasionally discusses tenets of other schools but most often as beliefs he is ready to give up in the light of discoveries of science. The Dalai Lama and other Buddhists who advocate the compatibility of true science and true Buddhism have the ear of the Western world. Less visible are other Tibetans, including abbots of major monasteries, who are not into this game. Perhaps, to them, the flexibility involved in the engagement with science has too high a price with respect to what they consider authentic Buddhism. The question of whether and how to align the tradition with modern science is one that marks the difference between reformers and traditionalists within Tibetan Buddhism, which is just as much a struggle as the culture wars over evolution in American Christianity.

As a cultural historian, the humanities scholar might thus be perceived as one who spoils the party, in this case the image of science-friendly Buddhism. Appeals to the natural sciences serve as instruments in a competition over authority to set the course for future Tibetan Buddhism. In the engagement with scientists, the discussion seems to deal with scientific issues, but scholars in the humanities such as Donald Lopez uncover complexities in categories used; they show us the diversity within those traditions and the multifaceted nature of interactions and translations. The unwelcome character of humanities scholarship may be especially pronounced when its scholarly study of traditional sources in their historical contexts is at odds with the engagement by diaspora communities, converts, or interested scientists who selectively appropriate materials and gurus, as the humanities scholars may signal that a particular appropriation is at odds with the meaning of the tradition and of the sources drawn upon.

Area studies itself has its setting in the academic landscape, even though it does not fit well within the main disciplinary structure within the humanities. Area studies encompasses many different disciplines, such as history, philosophy, religious studies, linguistics, and political sciences. It is itself not one more discipline alongside those disciplines, which is confusing for universities and funding agencies. In the humanities, one has departments of history, philosophy, linguistics, and so on, alongside China studies and Africa studies. If you want to study philosophy, you go to the department of philosophy, unless you want to do Chinese philosophy, which is to be found within China studies. We don't do the same for Dutch philosophy, German philosophy, British philosophy, or French philosophy, placing these with the study of Dutch, German, English, or French language and literature. For the expert on Chinese philosophy, institutionally the nearest colleagues are thus not other philosophers but experts on Chinese poetry and grammar.

The way we distinguish disciplines has arisen in the West. The structure of the disciplinary landscape shapes the methodologies and categories that have earned academic priority. Terminologies and methods typical of historical studies, cultural studies, or philosophy may be enriched by deep knowledge of developments in other parts of the world, but this is less likely to happen when knowledge of non-Western cultures is placed in a separate reserve, area studies. For practical reasons, such area studies might need to be separate because of the linguistic and cultural knowledge demanded to access the original texts. But positioning area studies alongside history, philosophy, and cultural studies suggests a difference between histories, philosophies and cultures that are ours and the histories and cultures of those others.[11]

It may be justified to give more attention to historical movements that have, to a large extent, shaped one's own world, and thus give priority to European philosophy in philosophy programs in Europe. However, that is not a scholarly consideration but a social one. Nor is it an innocent one, as it might gloss over the influence of those others on our culture; we write with Arabic numerals and owe the number

11 Carine Defoort and Nicolas Standaert, "Areastudies stellen wetenschappen ter discussie," *Onze Alma Mater* 51 (1997), 393–413; Carine Defoort, "De blinde vlekken van multidisciplinariteit: Een bespreking van Hoe word ik Einstein of Da Vinci?" *Ethische Perspectieven* 25 (2015), 275–287.

zero to India, to give some examples from mathematics. It makes the others exotic, and it might treat those others as all similar to each other, as if there were a homogeneous non-West, a typical Asia or a unified Arabic world, passing by the ways in which within such vast regions cultures vary from place to place, from group to group, from individual to individual.

The humanities seek to help understand others, their languages, and cultures. That is not easy. Many scholars are sensitive to differences across and within cultures, and to the potential for bias that comes with our own position, easily the yardstick by which others are judged. Thus, learning as good as we can their languages and their historical, social, and cultural contexts is an important contributions the humanities make to our vast human world. The risk of not understanding others correctly is even greater when we not only want to have knowledge *about* them, but intend to treat them as persons who might have to say something to us. Which brings us back to "hermeneutics," a term introduced in the opening chapter.

HERMENEUTICS: INTERPRETATION AS A HUMAN NECESSITY

Hermeneutics can be associated with the Greek god "Hermes," the god of travel, trade, and thieves. Hermes, similar to the Roman god Mercury, conveys messages of the gods. Statutes depict him as an athletic young man, with wings at his feet to indicate his speedy travels. The word hermeneutics goes back to a Greek verb that means to translate or to interpret.

The meaning of messages of the gods, prophesies, and oracles, has been disputed again and again. This issue is more general: Nothing is ever intelligible without knowledge of the context, and, even then, there is risk of misunderstanding. Lawyers and theologians have made "interpretation" their job. In biblical studies, one speaks of *exegesis*, understanding "out of" the text, but the risk is that one reads something into the text, attributing a meaning to it.

The term "hermeneutics" was applied in the seventeenth century to principles to be used in the exegesis of biblical texts, an important issue for European Protestants. Speaking of hermeneutics with respect to all communication between humans, and not merely as method in the interpretation of ancient texts, became important in the nineteenth century, due to the theologian Friedrich Schleiermacher (1766–1834). He distinguished grammatical and psychological interpretation. Grammatical interpretation is interpretation that focuses on the language itself, the meaning of words as given in dictionaries, the structure of sentences, and so on. Psychological interpretation focuses on the particular way words are used, revealing something about the speaker.

We also owe to Schleiermacher insights about *hermeneutical circles*. To understand a sentence, we have to read the words that make up the sentence. But we cannot understand those words, many of which may have multiple meanings, without considering the sentence in which they occur. Also, we cannot understand the sentence without paying attention to the text as a whole. But we don't know the meaning of the text as a whole, except by reading the sentences. When something is called gray, it makes a difference whether that is stated in the context of a treatise on colors, is said about the weather, or is used metaphorically to dismiss someone's contributions as boring. The word by itself is not enough to understand its meaning; we need to see the word in the context of the whole text. Understanding requires a back and forth between considering the whole and its parts. Many jokes and narratives play with this, introducing at the end of the story new elements that suddenly place the preceding words in an unexpected light.

Circularity regards not only words and sentences or larger texts. When we see at the bottom of an opinion piece who the author is, the meaning of a text might change. We come to see that the text reflects personal experience, serves self-interest or a political purpose, makes fun of opponents, or intends to do something else. Knowledge about the author may become a factor in determining the meaning of the words we just read. We need to know the speaker to understand the words, and we know the speaker by the words spoken, and by nonverbal clues we may notice but these need interpretation too.

The German term *Geisteswissenschaften* places the humanities within the sphere of the *Wissenschaften*, a term that is broader in meaning than the English term "sciences," which tends to refer to empirical and quantitative natural and social sciences. Within the broader field of science and scholarship, as *Wissenschaften*, the distinction between sciences and humanities was an important issue in the nineteenth century. Were they delivering similar kinds of knowledge?

An influential articulation of the character of the *Geisteswissenschaften* as different from the natural sciences was offered by Wilhelm Dilthey (1833–1911). If one were to discuss his work in reasonable depth, one would have to engage the German philosophical tradition, with Immanuel Kant who had articulated an influential view of the conditions for knowledge in the natural sciences, with Friedrich Schleiermacher, who influenced greatly the rise of hermeneutics as a general theory of human understanding, with Georg Wilhelm Friedrich Hegel, who had developed a view of history as the unfolding of the *Geist*, and with others in German Idealism and Romanticism. The following merely paraphrases some insights inspired by Dilthey and others, as insights that have been influential in the subsequent understanding of the humanities, without delving into their historical background.

Distinct from a scientific approach, with emphasis on quantification and explanation (*erklären*), in the humanities we seek a historical understanding that acknowledges the primacy of personal existence. In the quest to understand (*verstehen*), we seek to understand the "inner" meaning words and actions have to the actors involved. This is not about sharing their emotions or beliefs, but about insight into their attitudes and convictions. In this sense of knowledge, a friend might know me better than I know myself, and thus could know what I am going to say well before I started to speak.

The main distinction between the natural sciences and the humanities is not by domain, but by mode of knowing. The natural sciences seek to *explain* phenomena by seeing those as the result of a general law of nature. In doing so, there is a hierarchical pattern of disciplines – chemistry clearly builds upon physics. The coherence of reality, in the perspective of the natural sciences, shows itself in the relationships between different levels of analysis. This can be understood as an "outsider perspective" or third person perspective. There seems to be no "insider perspective" to the matter researched.

In some of his later work, Dilthey goes beyond a binary division of natural sciences and humanities. In the life sciences, such as biology and cognitive sciences, the interaction between an organism and its environment may be characterized by a sense of purpose of an organism, something more akin to an inner perspective than we find in the physical sciences. Dilthey articulates the tripartite division, with similarities across the disciplines as well as fundamental differences, as follows:[12]

> Self-evidently... the same elementary logical operations appear in the human and the natural sciences: induction, analysis, construction, and comparison. But what concerns us now is what special form they assume within the experiential domain of the humanities. Induction, whose data are sensory processes, proceeds here as everywhere on the basis of a knowledge of a connection. In the physical-chemical sciences this basis is the mathematical knowledge of quantitative relations; in the biological sciences it is the [nexus] of purposiveness [*Lebenszweckmäßigkeit*]; in the humanities it is the structure of psychic life.

Relationships between the various sciences would be a topic that needs a different book. Here, I just want to argue that we should avoid two extremes: an encompassing reduction, as if an analysis in physical, genetic, or evolutionary terms would do justice to human existence, and an unnecessary fear of reduction, as if our embodiment as material and biological beings would deny that we are thinking and feeling beings. The reductionism that characterizes the physical sciences is a form of holism, as it shows how different approaches fit together. But it is not sufficient nor adequate for the humanities.

In the humanities, multiple perspectives co-exist, supplementing each other, without a clear hierarchical structure. The humanities need to understand each event in its own context as meaningful to the person or persons involved. In doing so, one has to refer to humans with their intentions and ways of giving meaning to their world. We came across this distinction in the first chapter when the distinction between humans as agents and as actors was introduced – as causal factors, just as the weather may be an agent, and as persons whose

12 Wilhelm Dilthey quoted after Jos de Mul, "Leben erfasst hier Leben: Dilthey as a Philosopher of (the) Life (Sciences)," in Eric S. Nelson (ed.), *Interpreting Dilthey: Critical Essays* (Cambridge University Press, 2019), 41–60, p. 48; I translated "*Geisteswissenschaften*" as "humanities," rather than as "human sciences," as in De Mul's text.

actions may be understood in reference to motives and reasons, to the way they experience the world.

The focus is on life as lived; another German term used in this context, *Erlebnis*, speaks of a richer sense of "inner" experience, including desires and feelings that go beyond observation. The interest is in the individual and the particular; the biography is typically a genre that fits this orientation. Dilthey made his contribution with a biography of Friedrich Schleiermacher.

In his *Introduction to the Human Sciences*, originally from 1883, Dilthey contrasted his approach to previous philosophers who had considered the nature of knowledge.[13] They had

> explained experience and cognition in terms of facts that are merely representational. No real blood flows in the veins of the knowing subject constructed by Locke, Hume, and Kant, but rather the diluted extract of reason as a mere activity of thought. A historical as well as psychological approach to whole human beings led me to explain even knowledge and its concepts (such as the external world, time, substance, and cause) in terms of the manifold powers of a being that wills, feels, and thinks.

This research orientation emphasizes the richness of experience, of life as lived, which is considered richer than typical for the natural sciences and for the philosophers who merely focus on rationality.

The emphasis on human experience implies also certain self-imposed restrictions. As Jos de Mul wrote in his analysis of Dilthey, "The analysis of the nature and scope of experiential knowledge also requires a critique of the experience-transcending – that is, metaphysical – presumptions of reason"[14]. The word *Geist* may evoke for some readers the idea of a soul, the "Geist" as an entity separate from the body, and hence suggest a dualistic anthropology, but such a metaphysics is not in line with the emphasis on life as lived, which involves the whole person. This understanding of the humanities is in line with understanding humans as bodily, social, and cultural beings.

13 Dilthey, *Introduction to the Human Sciences. Wilhelm Dilthey, Selected Works, Volume I* (Princeton University Press 1989), p. 50.

14 De Mul, *The Tragedy of Finitude: Dilthey's Hermeneutics of Life* (New Haven: Yale University Press, 2004), p. 264.

Dilthey, himself the son of a reformed minister, had initially studied theology. But for theology too, he argues, we should turn to life as lived rather than take dogma as statements about God. Everything in life can become an object of religious value. Attributing such value presupposes relevant experiences within our lives. Religion serves to deal with the challenges of life, its frailty and vulnerability, and the desire for a solid basis, for trust, for peace. In poetry, art, religion, and philosophy human experiences in life are the basis for going beyond those experiences. The particular character of religion is that life as experienced is understood as standing in relation to the invisible, but the religious genius is not to be praised for dreams about another world, but about the persistence of life in the midst of suffering and joy. Dilthey rejects religion as knowledge about a transcendent reality; he is interested in the way a religious orientation shapes our experiential lives.

With some later authors such as Martin Heidegger (1889–1976), one might speak of *existential* hermeneutics, as it is not merely about the way we understands the world, but about the way we are ("exist") in the world. One of his students, Hans Georg Gadamer (1900–2002), reformulated the idea of hermeneutical circles by speaking of a speaker or text with its horizon, and me as a reader with my horizon, shaped by my history, my tradition. Understanding arises, and is transformative, when horizons merge, *Horizontverschmeltzung*. Prejudice is unavoidable, as we always live within a particular horizon. Understanding cannot arise if there is not already a preliminary understanding. Approaches that stress the way we are bounded to a particular horizon or tradition, have occasionally been used to support a conservative agenda. However, merging horizons may be transformative, as we transcend the limitations of our current point of view, even though our new point of view will have limitations too.[15]

In this very brief tour of hermeneutics, let me introduce one French thinker alongside the Germans. Paul Ricoeur (1913–2005) considered symbols. Some aspire to be univocal, as traffic signs or symbols in logic and mathematics. Many are equivocal; they have more than one

15 Richard E. Palmer, *Hermeneutics: Interpretation Theory in Schleiermacher, Dilthey, Heidegger, and Gadamer* (Evanston, IL: Northwestern University Press, 1969).

meaning. In his book *The Symbolism of Evil*, he reflects on the ways people have spoken of evil, in terms of defilement, of sin, and of guilt.[16] These ways of speaking are associated with various myths. The concluding section of Ricoeur's book is titled "The symbol gives rise to thought." The history of humanity, its philosophical, religious, and artistic expressions, is full of symbols and myths, of equivocal language. Some might dismiss these stories as primitive, for instance the biblical ones about the first humans, Adam and Eve, and about the first fratricide, of Abel by Cain; we now know better. Not only science contributes to such a critical attitude, but also the cultural and philosophical "masters of suspicion" such as Friedrich Nietzsche, Karl Marx, and Sigmund Freud, thinkers who explained what people say and believe in terms alien to those of the people involved. Ricoeur appreciates their critical thinking as a gift of modernity. But alongside the critical approach, he suggests, we should use constructively myths and symbols. We should take those myths seriously, though not literally but in a "second naiveté." Again, one might discern a hermeneutic circle, a back and forth between explanatory critical thought and engagement with that which is meaningfully expressed in symbols and myths. Also, one might add, so too for other human expressions, in literature and art, in music, movies, advertisements, and ordinary language.

But if we appropriate the symbols and texts of others, make them our own, do we do justice to those others? In the next section, we will consider the emphasis on the author's intent, and illustrate its critical potential by considering the development of biblical studies.

AUTHORIAL INTENT AS A SCHOLARLY NORM

Interpretation is risky. We might be mistaken about the meaning we attribute to the words of another. Can we ever know that our interpretation is right? Is there a correct interpretation? What would be the norm? Is the hermeneutical circle, the back and forth between details and the text as a whole, not making interpretation like the task of

16 Paul Ricoeur, *The Symbolism of Evil* (New York: Harper & Row, 1967).

Sisyphus, rolling the stone up the hill again and again, never to be completed? Or, at least, is one interpretation never better than another interpretation, as we cannot step outside the circle of interpretations, as there is no norm beyond the text?

As one major normative strategy, we will focus in this section on interpretations that seek stability by treating as the norm the intentions of the author and the meaning of the text in its original context. A strategy that focuses on the initial historical context can be considered scholarly well-defined and safe. However, it may generate substantial tension with readers at a later time, for whom the text has become significant but who have come to understand it differently. We'll illustrate this with examples from the development of biblical studies. But first, let us introduce the strategy by considering work of one advocate of the focus on original meaning.

E. D. Hirsch, Jr., is an American educator, who has stressed the importance of knowledge, and not merely "critical skills." He is also a literary critic, and wrote about this discipline in *Validity in Interpretation* and *The Aims of Interpretation*. A distinction he makes in those books is between the meaning of a text and its significance. When seeking knowledge, we should seek to understand the *meaning* of the text, as the meaning that reflects the intention of the author, for the audience for which the text was originally intended. Thus, as he sees it, there is a historical norm; the meaning was fixed when the text was written. It is there to be discovered; one can offer arguments why a particular interpretation might be plausible, given the original audience, and why another interpretation might be implausible. Reconstructing the meaning of a text involves a reasoned guess about what the author might have meant. It is a creative process, but it has a definite focus.

Significance may sound soft, as significant for me, a reader at a later time. However, according to Hirsch, a later reader who finds significance is also someone operating in a particular context, a context in which questions are posed or values may be operative that differ from those of the author and the originally intended audience. This may even be in relation to the author when rereading earlier work, and judging it to be inadequate: the meaning has not changed, but precisely because that meaning was fixed when the work was written, its significance for the author may have changed, as the author has come to experience the world differently.[17]

If I apply this to biblical studies, an historical-critical approach would seek to reconstruct the original meaning, whereas reception history is more about the significance the text had for later people, in other contexts. But within each context, there is a similar objectivity about the meaning the text has for the people involved. Significance, too, is to be understood in relation to a particular context. If one studies the way a text is used at a later moment, say in a particular religious community, one may be interested in the meaning it receives in that community, rather than the meaning it had for the initial author. However, unless stated differently, meaning is the meaning it had when the text was written.

Hirsch considers the focus on authorial intent a moral and intellectual choice. If the goal were just to pass time by inventing possible interpretations, anything might count. Also, if the goal were to establish God's Kingdom on Earth, only a politically engaged reading might be acceptable. But such ways of reading are determined by personal preferences of the reader, rather than by scholarly criteria. The only norm for discerning the meaning of a text that would not make the meaning of the text depend upon personal interests of the reader, is the meaning the author intended to convey to the original audience in the original context. Also, of course, if one seeks to establish the meaning of a text in relation to its context, it is important to have the original text. Thus, such an attitude toward texts stimulated philological research and the creation of critical editions that reconstruct as much as possible the original version of a text.

Understanding the meaning of a text as its meaning in the original context, as intended by its author, is academically a clear strategy. Its results may be controversial, as it may be at odds with the way texts have been handed down through time and are understood at a later time. We will consider this in two case studies, on Christianity and on Hinduism. Before doing so, we'll complete the general reflection on interpretative strategies, understanding others, with a brief discussion of a different way of thinking about interpretation, one that does not

17 E. D. Hirsch, Jr., *Validity in Interpretation* (New Haven: Yale University Press, 1967), p. 7f.; E. D. Hirsch Jr., *The Aims of Interpretation* (University of Chicago Press, 1976).

make the original setting decisive. The key is that the meaning of a text relates to the reader, also the reader at a later time. We don't read texts just to understand the past.

HEARERS AND READERS

Whereas the scholarly orientation considered above, fairly natural to the historically minded, is to consider the meaning of a text the meaning in its original context, there are other orientations within the humanities. Not all humanities scholars are historians, nor are they so all the time.

If an author sends a novel or poem into the world, it may come to mean what it will mean to its future readers. The American literary critic, Stanley Fish, author of *Is There a Text in This Class?*, thinks along such lines.[18] Fish writes that he used to assume a clear distinction between the text, the author, and the readers, but now has come to reject that view. Initially, he thought that the focus of interpretation should be the text, as the intentions of the author are not accessible, and the responses of readers may vary too much. However, he now gives priority to the *act of reading*, as a text does not exist in a complete form except in the act of being read as a text. Also, as reading takes time, the meaning of the text is not determined until the act of reading is completed; the final sentences may change the meaning a text has for us.

But not all readers have the same competences and interests. One option might be to think about the meaning for a linguistically competent ideal reader. By assuming an ideal reader, we might hope to have stability of meaning, However, this would not do justice to the variation among readers. It would come at the price of passing by diversity and genuine human involvement, suppressing the subjective and idiosyncratic that characterizes humans.

Fish emphasizes that a reader does not exist without an interpretative community that has shaped our thinking and understanding. Meaning is not subjective and private; the discourse on valid

18 Stanley C. Fish, *Is There a Text in This Class? The Authority of Interpretative Communities* (Cambridge, MA: Harvard University Press, 1980).

interpretations refers to meanings that are public, though related to a particular community and context. If a student raises a hand in class at a university, this may signal that this student would like to make a comment or raise a question. If a student does so in elementary school, it might mean that the pupil seeks permission to go to the bathroom. If in a university classroom, the action "raising a hand" were interpreted as physical exercise rather than as a request, it would be highly unlikely that the interpretation would be right, in that particular community and context.

Actions and words are interpreted in relation to a context, and can be judged as probably true or false on the basis of the assumptions shared in that particular community. By emphasizing the community of the one who tries to understand someone else's words or actions, Fish focuses on the subject who interprets, more than on the text. As Fish sees it, discussion to determine which interpretation is plausible, is about persuasion of others in the community, rather than about argumentation.

In her book *Uses of Literature*, Rita Felski addresses in particular the reading of literature.[19] She is interested in the impact a novel might have, how it may "infiltrate and inform our lives." This is in relation to not only ordinary readers, but also literary critics and scholars in literary or cultural studies. Focusing on the historical origin of the text passes by important other questions.

> One consequence of such historical embedding is that the critic is absolved of the need to think through her own relationship to the text she is reading. Why has this work been chosen for interpretation? How does it speak to me now? What is its value in the present? To focus only on the work's origins is to side-step the question of its appeal to the present-day reader. . . . Yet the cumulative force of its past associations, connotations, and effects by no means exhausts a work's power of address. What of its ability to transverse temporal boundaries and to generate new and unanticipated resonances, including those that cannot be predicted by its original circumstances?

19 Rita Felski, *Uses of Literature* (Malden, MA: Blackwell, 2008), quotes from pp. 5, 10, and 14.

According to her, even the scholar who prioritizes original intent has to face questions regarding his own choices, and thus the way the text is read at a later time. In subsequent chapters she proposes "that reading involves a logic of *recognition*; that aesthetic experience has analogies with *enchantment* in a supposedly disenchanted age; that literature creates distinctive configurations of social *knowledge*; that we may value the experience of being *shocked* by what we read." These are different forms of engagement with the text read, relating the texts to ourselves, in the processes of self-formation we are involved in.

So much for a brief tour of reflections on the way we interpret texts, and thereby understand others and ourselves. This is not merely an issue for scholars, nor one for individuals reading novels. Disputes on the way we approach texts may be consequential and controversial. Within Western Christianity, scholarly pressure to focus on the text in its original context has been transformative; *ad fontes*, back to the original sources, became a rallying cry for Protestant Christianity. We will consider here in a case study what this did for the engagement with texts. A second case study will be on a particular book on Hinduism, written by a Western scholar, which became controversial to some Hindus. Who is allowed to interpret Hinduism? What is genuine Hinduism? Normative issues are tied up with processes of interpretation of the history of a tradition.

CASE STUDY (1): CHRISTIANITY

A turn to the original meaning characterizes scholarship in the humanities at least since the Renaissance. During the Renaissance, interest in the reconstruction of texts from Antiquity developed. Scholars noted variants, as one manuscript might have a slightly different version of a text than another manuscript. Such differences may have arisen unintentionally due to copying errors. Variants may also have been introduced intentionally when a copyist inserted explications or corrected what seemed to the copyist a mistake of a previous copyist. Humans are fallible, and so, too, are copyists and translators. Creating text editions that reconstruct the original version and document carefully the various variants, has been central to philological scholarship, on texts from Greek and Roman Antiquity and other sources. It became an important preliminary to substantial historical analysis and modern interpretations – especially if one seeks interpretations that correspond with authorial intent.

Desiderius Erasmus (1466?–1536), an erudite biblical humanist, in 1516 published a new, annotated Latin translation of the New Testament, with an edition of the Greek text on the opposite pages. His scholarly edition differed from the Latin translation that was accepted by the Church, the Vulgate. In the Vulgate, translated once more into English, a passage in one of the Letters of the New Testament, 1 John 5, verses 7 and 8, reads as follows:

> For there are three that beare record *in heaven, the Father, the Word, and the Holy Ghost: and these three are one. And there are three that beare witnesse on earth*, the Spirit, and the Water and the Blood, and these three agree in one
>
> (italics added)

This text was support for the Christian doctrine of the Trinity, which understands God as one and undivided, but known as the Father, the Son, and the Holy Spirit. The text italicized here, on the witnesses in heaven, became known as the Comma Johanneum, the Johannine clause. "The Word" refers to Jesus Christ, of whom the opening verses of the Gospel of John speak of as "the Logos." Speaking of these three as one, affirmed the doctrine of the Trinity – three but one.

Erasmus had found no evidence for the Comma Johanneum in the Greek manuscripts he had consulted. Thus, he left the italicized passage out of his edition of the Greek sources and also out of his new Latin translation. This decision by Erasmus caused concern by those who relied on the Bible to support their theological views and ecclesiastical authority. Erasmus seemed to promote a theological heresy, or at least to allow for one.

His critics must have been relieved when a few years later in England a Greek manuscript was discovered that did have the Comma Johanneum. In 1522 Erasmus included the Trinitarian passage in his third edition of the New Testament in Greek and Latin. In an annotation, he wrote: "I therefore restored from the British codex what was said to be lacking in our editions, lest anyone should have any handle to blame me unjustly. However, I suspect that this codex was adapted to agree with the manuscripts of the Latins." By adding the Trinitarian clause, Erasmus saved his Latin translation and Greek edition from suspicions of heresy, which otherwise for his work might have had negative consequences for its market and in the Church. Theological orthodoxy seemed safe again. No minor matter in a time of religious turmoil; the Protestant Reformation is taken to have started in 1517 with the ninety-five theses of Martin Luther nailed to the door of a church in Wittenberg.

The British codex served remarkably well to counter a theologically unwelcome philological reconstruction of the "original" text of the Bible. Though Erasmus had reintroduced the Trinitarian clause, the Comma Johanneum remained contested. Recently, Grantley McDonald has analyzed the manuscripts and scholarly and theological debates and argued that for these verses the newly found Greek manuscript, now known as the Codex Montfortianus, was a translation from Latin into Greek, and that its scribe had had access to Erasmus's 1516 edition of the New Testament. Hence, by scholarly standards, it is a late invention, likely to have been written with the intention to have Erasmus change his edition.[20]

Critical editions, such as the edition of the Greek New Testament by Erasmus, seek to establish the original text and study the variants that have arisen over time. They focus on the intent of the author, or of a text in its initial context, which is scholarly a fairly clear strategy that keeps personal preferences at bay. However, focusing on history may make the process of interpretation of texts vulnerable to changing historical knowledge about the author and the original context in which the text arose.

20 Grantley McDonald, *Biblical Criticism in Early Modern Europe: Erasmus, the Johannine Comma and the Trinitarian Debate* (Cambridge University Press, 2016); Erasmus is quoted from p. 319; the remark about the commercial interest is inspired by p. 29, and by Henk Jan De Jonge, "Comma Johanneum," in *Religion in Geschichte und Gegenwart,* Vierte Auflage, Band 2, p. 429. The text of 1 John 5:7-8 according to the Authorized Version of 1611, is quoted from p.62 of McDonald, "The Johannine Comma from Erasmus to Westminster," in D. van Miert, H. Nellen, P. Steenbakkers, and J. Touber (eds.), *Scriptural Authority and Biblical Criticism in the Dutch Golden Age: God's Word Questioned* (Oxford University Press, 2017), 61–72.

Tradition had it that Moses had been the author of the first five books of the Bible, known in Judaism as the *Torah* and in Christianity as the first five books of the Old Testament, the *Pentateuch*. In his *Tractatus Theologico-Politicus*, published in 1670, Baruch or Benedict Spinoza – a philosopher and Jew banned by the synagogue in Amsterdam – argued that Moses could not have been the author of those books. Whereas in the example of the Johannine Comma the text as passed through the centuries since its origin was in dispute, giving rise to the philological activity called "text criticism" or "lower criticism," here we see a discussion on the origin of the texts, what came to be called "higher criticism" or historical-critical studies. To counter a potential misunderstanding: "critical" is not intended as negative, criticism, but as careful evaluation.

Spinoza's work was dismissed as "a book forged in hell," as if written by the devil himself, since it treated the Bible as a book that could be studied just as any other human work. As Samuel Preus argued in *Spinoza and the Irrelevance of Biblical Authority* "the rise of the study of religion required a more fundamental alteration: the Bible's uniquely privileged (*i.e.*, canonical) status had to be set aside entirely in order to open the way for comparing the Bible with other ancient texts, and the biblical religions with other religions around the world. I maintain that Spinoza was the first to accomplish this."[21]

Unlike Preus, others emphasized continuity with preceding scholarship. Nicholas Hardy wrote in his *Criticism and Confession: The Bible in the Seventeenth Century Republic of Letters* on the continuity between insights from the humanist era and subsequent Enlightenment biblical criticism such as Spinoza's. The challenge to Moses as author was not new, but it became subversive due to the way Spinoza used those arguments. Scholarly continuity is also defended by Anthony Grafton, who extensively studied Joseph Scaliger, a major philological scholar in the late sixteenth and early seventeenth century, over half a century before Spinoza. Scaliger already concluded that humans had made deliberate changes to the text of the Bible. Grafton

21 Benedictus de Spinoza, *Theological-Political Treatise* (Cambridge University Press, 2007); Steven M. Nadler, *A Book Forged in Hell: Spinoza's Scandalous Treatise and the Birth of the Secular Age* (Princeton University Press, 2011); J. Samuel Preus, *Spinoza and the Irrelevance of Biblical Authority* (Cambridge University Press, 2001), p. ix.

thus writes: "Spinoza pulled together ideas that had already been widely diffused, clarified their implications, and gave them a dramatic new expression."

In contrast, Jonathan Israel, another scholar of the period emphasizes discontinuity. "The revolutionary character of Spinoza's hermeneutic has important implications for the way we evaluate the advances in scholarship in the later seventeenth century." There were precursors, but none of these "went so far as Spinoza in undermining the entire procedure of citing Scripture to underpin the broad theological claims that formed such a staple element of early modern culture."[22]

Given the standing of Jonathan Israel, known for major works such as *Radical Enlightenment: Philosophy and the Making of Modernity, 1650–1750*, one may understand the title of Grafton's contribution, "An heretical approach," as ironic. He positions his own contribution as heretical, relative to a dominant position in the *scholarly* discussions. Both Grafton and Israel are experts on the debates of the time and have studied original sources. Their difference in assessing the significance of Spinoza shows us something about the humanities: Even when scholars agree on the data, they may present those in different ways, depending on the questions and assumptions they as scholars bring to the material. But despite the different assessment on the novelty of this attitude, they both agree that the turn toward an understanding of the text in its historical context is the way to go.

A historically informed revision of our understanding of the texts is offensive to some readers. The continuing development of historical-critical studies of the Bible and new awareness of "deep time" in the course of the nineteenth century generated further tensions. Such scholarship became one of the decisive factors in the split between modern and traditional believers, the rise of fundamentalism and the resistance to it.

22 Nicholas Hardy, *Criticism and Confession: The Bible in the Seventeenth Century Republic of Letters* (Oxford University Press, 2017); Anthony Grafton, "Spinoza's Hermeneutics: Some Heretical Thoughts," in *Scriptural Authority and Biblical Criticism in the Dutch Golden Age*, 177–196, p. 187; Jonathan Israel, "How Did Spinoza Declare War on Theology and Theologians?," same volume, 197–216; quotes pp. 197, 199.

Efforts to understand biblical texts in their historical context accelerated in the nineteenth century with new discoveries in the Middle East. In 1872, George Smith, a self-taught assistant at the British Museum, studying clay tablets excavated a few decades earlier, wrote: "my eye caught the statement that the ship rested upon the mountains of Nizir, followed by the account of the sending forth of the dove, and its finding no resting-place and returning. I saw at once that I had here discovered a portion at least of the Chaldean account of the Deluge." The Gilgamesh epos, as the narrative that included this passage came to be known, at first seemed to support the veracity of the biblical story of Noah and the Flood, told in the first book of the Bible, Genesis. It later became evident that the biblical story had been adapted from stories such as the Gilgamesh epic, which may have predated the biblical narrative by a millennium. With such insights, but also due to developments in geology and other disciplines, came a broader cultural awareness of "deep time," with substantial consequences for the Victorian self-understanding.[23]

Other insights about precursors of biblical text emerged through careful analysis of the language of the Hebrew Bible. Scholars came to the hypothesis that there had been multiple authors in the first five books, including Genesis, each with their own style and concerns, and writing within a different historical setting. One, labelled by scholars J, referred to God as JHWH and had a particular interest in the Kingdom of Juda, while another, E, referred to God as Elohim and showed more interest in the kingdom of Israel. A third one, D, was focusing on the law, Deuteronomy, while a fourth, P, gave priority to priestly practices, often related to the Temple. At some point, an editor (Redactor, R) has woven various precursors into a single whole.

In the later part of the Bible, the New Testament, the gospels of Mark. Matthew and Luke show overlap in various ways. The main hypothesis became that Mark is the oldest text, known to the authors of Matthew and Luke; that Matthew and Luke shared another source (in scholarly German "*Quelle*," Q), while each also had material particular to that author. Thus, a tapestry of oral transmission and

23 Stephen Mitchell, *Gilgamesh: A New English Version* (New York: Free Press, 2004), p. 4; also, Vybarr Cregan-Reid, *Discovering Gilgamesh: Geology, Narrative and the Historical Sublime in Victorian Culture* (Manchester University Press, 2013), p. 39.

precursors has been hypothesized, preceding the New Testament that became normative for Christianity.

Biblical scholarship treats texts as the work of humans, speaking in their own particular voices and with their own particular interests, to audiences in their own time. Those texts were revised and integrated into a single whole by editors who also had their particular preferences. Thus, the Bible and the tradition were humanized, as expressions of convictions and practices of humans witnessing in their historical contexts. Rather than approaching the Holy Book as written by the divine Author, it was the creation of human authors.

In parallel to this scholarly development in the nineteenth century, to paint the picture with broad strokes, we see the rise of liberal variants of Christianity that are willing to accept religious scripture as human testimony, as well as the rise of anti-modernist, "evangelical" forms of Christianity, stressing confessional identity and biblical inerrancy. Though the subsequent rise of fundamentalism has become associated with opposition to an evolutionary understanding of the natural world, the rise of a historical understanding of the Bible has been at least as important, if not more. Jonathan Israel spoke of three main components in the intellectual European development in the modern period, in science, philosophy, and humanistic scholarship. The last one has received least attention from historians, but it may have been the most influential of the three. One might even argue that it was humanistic scholarship that, a few centuries earlier, facilitated the rise of modern science, as Peter Harrison has argued in his *The Bible, Protestantism, and the Rise of Natural Science.*[24]

Historical studies may be challenging to interpretations that have been dear to believers in earlier ages, and also to some today, as these identify themselves with the believers of an earlier age. Modernist believers who accept that the meaning of the text is to be understood historically as the meaning in its original context while taking the liberty to decide on its significance for today differently, need not have much trouble with new insights into the texts. For the scholar, dealing with new understandings of the past is, of course, part of the job

24 Peter Harrison, *The Bible, Protestantism and the Rise of Natural Science* (Cambridge University Press, 1998).

description. But a choice for such a scholarly approach may have a philosophical and political agenda as well, as when Spinoza in the seventeenth century offered his arguments about the Bible in the context of the *Theological-Political Treatise*, a book that in later chapters argued for a democratic and religiously pluralist state. Politics is also at stake in a recent controversy on Hinduism.

CASE STUDY (2): THE HINDUS

Early in 2014, Penguin Books India announced that, in a settlement to avoid a legal challenge, they would recall and destroy all remaining copies of *The Hindus: An Alternative History*. The author of the book was Wendy Doniger, professor of the history of religions at the University of Chicago. Why? According to an article on the decision of Penguin Books India, Doniger writes that she "wanted to tell a story of Hinduism that's been suppressed and was increasingly hard to find in the media and textbooks, ... It's not about philosophy, it's not about meditation, it's about stories, about animals and untouchables and women. It's the way that Hinduism has dealt with pluralism."[25]

Doniger's book has almost 700 pages of text and hundreds of footnotes referring to original sources and scholarly literature. The author offers an extensive and well documented history, from traces of early humans on the Indian subcontinent to Hinduism in our time. Throughout the book, she returns to ideas about sexuality and women, to ideas about animals, especially cows, dogs, and horses, and to opinions on violence and nonviolence. On these themes, she offers insights that deviate from the customary image of Hinduism in India and in the Western diaspora.

She provides textual evidence that in early Hinduism animals were sacrificed and that their meat was eaten, including the beef of cows, though mostly these were kept for milk. It is only gradually that in many strands of Hinduism animal sacrifices were banned. As she quotes from the *Jaiminiya Brahmana*, composed around 600 BCE:

25 John Williams, "Author Resigned to Ill Fate of Book in India," *New York Times* (February 17, 2014), C1; Wendy Doniger, "Banned in Bangalore," *New York Times* (March 5, 2014), A29.

> In the beginning, the skin of cattle was the skin that humans have now, and the skin of humans was the skin cattle have now. Cattle could not bear the heat, rain, flies, and mosquitoes. They went to humans and said, "Let this skin be yours and that skin be ours." "What would be the result of that?" humans asked. "You could eat us," said the cattle, "and this skin of ours would be your clothing."

Over time, not eating beef acquired the symbolic significance it has today, especially when it served to demarcate Hindus from Muslims, with whom they share the Indian subcontinent.

Doniger points out the sexual character of various symbols. A text from the Upanishads "analogizes a woman's genitals to the sacrificial fire: Her vulva is the fire wood, her pubic hair the smoke, her vagina the flame; the acts of penetration and climax are the embers and the sparks." She discerns two major strands within Hinduism, the sensual artistic imagery and poetry of worldly Hindus and the puritanism of various Hindu sects, especially those withdrawing from the world. As she writes, the currently dominant puritan attitudes have been strengthened by the colonial period. "When confronting the earthier aspects of Hinduism, such as the worship of the linga, the British were not amused. And some nineteenth-century Hindu movements internalized British Protestant – indeed Victorian – scorn for Hindu eroticism and polytheism."

Nor are ideals of nonviolence as clear and ancient as one might think. Mahatma Gandhi drew on select elements of the tradition when standing up against the British. But his nonviolence failed against the violence that erupted after independence, leading to the split of Pakistan and India. Doniger suggests that Gandhi's nonviolence disregarded another deep Hindu ideal. "For as Krishna pointed out in the *Bhagavad Gita*, it is quite possible to adhere to the mental principles of non-violence while killing your cousins in battle."[26]

Throughout the book, Doniger emphasizes that Hinduism is diverse and dynamic rather than homogeneous, with major disagreements between strands within Hinduism. So much for this quick tour of some highlights of this scholarly book. This book became

26 Doniger, *The Hindus: An Alternative History* (New York: Viking Penguin, 2009), pp. 135, 177, 597f., and 627.

controversial, resulting in the publisher in India withdrawing the book. How? Why?

Dina Nath Batra, the former director of a Hindu-nationalist organization in India, filed a complaint. The main legal basis was section 295A of the Indian Penal Code:

> Whoever, with deliberate and malicious intention of outraging the religious feelings of any class of citizens of India, by words, either spoken or written, or by signs or by visible representations or otherwise, insults or attempts to insult the religion or the religious beliefs of that class, shall be punished with imprisonment of either description for a term which may extend to three years, or with fine, or with both.

Thus, the claim that a particular group feels offended is by itself sufficient. This legal article goes back to the period of British rule. Batra mentioned five specific examples that caused such offense. Doniger had called the *Rāmāyaṇa* a "work of fiction"; her suggestion that the female hero in this epic, Sita, had sex with the brother of Rama was "pure and total blasphemy"; Doniger had now translated a passage of the *Rig Veda* as being about cows, whereas previously she had spoken of the sacrifice of cattle; and she had characterized the impregnation of Kunti, the mother of five heroes and kings in the other great epic, the *Mahābhārata* as "rape." The book's cover was also offensive, as it depicted "Lord Krishna ... sitting on the buttocks of a naked woman surrounded by other naked women" as "invading the sacredness attached to Sri Krishna." Given the Indian Penal Code, Penguin Books India agreed to the settlement, while it was also concerned about the safety of its employees. However, no copies of the book have been destroyed, as the book had sold out quickly. Digital copies circulated widely, and since then, another publisher has bought the rights and re-issued the book in India.[27]

27 Brian K. Pennington, "The Unseen Hand of an Underappreciated Law: The Doniger Affair and Its Aftermath." *Journal of the American Academy of Religion* 84 (2016), 323–336, pp. 324 and 326f. C. S. Adcock, "Violence, Passion, and the Law: A Brief History of Section 295A and Its Antecedents." *Journal of the American Academy of Religion* 84 (2016), 337–351. On republication in India: Doniger, "The Fight for the History of Hinduism in the Academy," in W. Doniger and M. C. Nussbaum (eds.), *Pluralism and Democracy in India: Debating the Hindu Right* (Oxford University Press, 2015), 310–326.

Though the legal challenge played out in India, some Hindus in the United States of America fueled the controversy. An example is *Academic Hinduphobia: A Critique of Wendy Doniger's Erotic School of Indology*, by Rajiv Malhotra. He objects to issues of a general nature. Doniger distinguished three such issues:

1. Non-Hindus rather than Hindus are writing about Hinduism;
2. Some non-Hindus (and indeed some Hindus, too) are writing about the "wrong sort" of Hinduism; and
3. Prominent authors, non-Hindu or Hindu, are writing from an academic rather than a faith stance.

If one were to expect non-Hindus to write from a faith stance, this would probably be perceived as judgmental or missionary rather than as respectful. The academic stance is the more neutral option available. However, by not being bound to a faith-based interpretation of the canon of Hinduism, it may indeed consider varieties of Hinduism and texts that deviate from Hinduism as considered canonical by a particular group of adherents, to them the wrong sort of Hinduism. Perhaps even more objectionable, the author might offer of the core texts of Hinduism an understanding different from the one they consider orthodox.

Doniger sees activist Hindutva Hinduism as just one among many strands, and not as the pure, original, and indigenous version of venerable antiquity, their self-image. According to her, Hindutva Hinduism is a modern phenomenon, owing much to the influence of the British.[28]

> Many of the Hindu elite who worked closely with the British caught the prejudices of their masters. In the 19th century, those Hindus lifted up other aspects of Hinduism – its philosophy, its tradition of meditation – that were more palatable to European tastes and made them into a new, sanitized brand of Hinduism, often referred to as

28 J. E. Llewellyn, "Think Globally, Get Death Threats Locally: The Politics of Studying Hinduism," in: W. Braun and R. T. McCutcheon (eds.), *Introducing Religion: Studies in Honor of Jonathan Z. Smith* (London: Equinox, 2008), 282–295; Rajiv Malhotra, *Academic Hinduphobia: A Critique of Wendy Doniger's Erotic School of Indology* (New Delhi: Voice of India, 2016); Doniger, "The Fight for the History of Hinduism in the Academy"; passage quoted from Doniger, "Banned in Bangalore."

> Sanatana Dharma, "the Eternal Law." That's the Hinduism that Hindutva-vadis are defending, while they deny the one that the Christian missionaries hated and that I love and write about – the pluralistic, open-ended, endlessly imaginative, often satirical Hinduism. The Hindutva-vadis are the ones who are attacking Hinduism; I am defending it against them.

The scholar need not be in line with the self-understanding of the orthodox in our time. Thereby, the insights of the scholar may become an issue among the believers involved. In this case, the historian of a religious practice offers a description of a tradition that is at odds with the self-understanding of a major group of practitioners. Doniger is not anti-religious, but she challenges their understanding of Hinduism and offers as an alternative a broader outlook on religions. In contrast to her historically informed account of the tradition, her opponents argue that their normative version of Hinduism should be guiding our interpretation of the past, and hence, that the only ones who are entitled to describe Hinduism are Hindus, and even more, Hindus of the right orientation.

UNDERSTANDING OTHERS – AND REFLECTING UPON OURSELVES

The humanities are about humans, their languages and cultures. *Our* languages and cultures. Understanding the author of a text, the creator of a piece of art, my neighbor in a conversation, a peasant or an emperor from Roman times, may be a challenge. However, we owe it to other humans to attempt to understand them as they aim to be understood. Scholarly interpretation seeks to understand texts and other materials in relation to the speaker or author, the initial context, and the intended audience. Even then, however, interpretation is a creative process, an attempt to understand. Interpretation can also arise in a broader human context. Its purpose need not be to understand what the text meant for the author, but rather may involve us, later readers. How does inspire a text or a work of art us to experience the world?

Interpretations may be relevant. To what extent is a judge bound by the original meaning of a law? If marriage at the time of the framers of the American Constitution was about a man and a woman, should it still be understood thus? The tension between original meaning and meaning for us at a later time, is one that can be acknowledged by scholars, but has to be handled by judges and other professionals in law, as well as by religious leaders who appeal to texts from a distant past, while addressing social and technological challenges that have arisen in our time. In Chapter 5, we will develop this theme, on originalism and living interpretation, when we discuss interpretation in such professional contexts, rather than as a purely academic pursuit.

Though the humanities seek to understand others, it is not just about others. In the engagement with others, we also come to reflect upon ourselves. That dimension of the humanities will be central to the next chapter.

3

Self-involving

Philosophy and Theology

SO FAR, WE HAVE FOCUSED ON HUMANITIES AS DISCIPLINARY efforts to understand *other* humans, their lives, languages, and literatures. However, what we learn about others we may apply to ourselves. Our predicament is like that of medical students who learn about diseases patients may have, and in the process start to wonder about their own health. But in the humanities, this self-reflective side is not merely a psychological effect of the knowledge acquired. When we encounter others, we might wonder how am I able to get "into their heads"? Who am I, the one who is engaging those others? Is their way of experiencing the world comprehensible to me? Would it appeal to me? Do their norms apply to me? The humanities involve ourselves as humans, as *subjects*. If we try to grasp how others experience the social and cultural world, participate in it, and thereby contribute to it, we assume them to be humans, who have inner lives just as we do. In the process, we are involved as humans who bring with us our own assumptions and frames when we create our knowledge of those others.

Self-involvement is particularly pronounced in theology and philosophy, disciplines that address our identities and the validity of our ideas. However, self-involvement characterizes the humanities more generally. A scholar who studies a particular culture, interacts with insiders to whom it might be their life-world. Those insiders would like to have their culture accepted, rather than merely observed and described. As we aspire to be scholars guided by academic norms, we cannot but be insiders to academic culture. We bring with us concepts and affective biases from our own cultural context. As Mary Fulbrook made clear in her book *Historical Theory*, even in a relatively "objective" branch of the humanities, history, the scholar is intimately involved in the research, as we do investigate the past from the present. The three parts of her book express this well in their titles:

I. Interpretations: Approaches to History;
II. Investigations: Routes from the Present to the Past;
III. Representations: The Past in the Present.

It is from the present that we form ideas about the past, and thereby represent the past in our present, perhaps to convey a moral message or strengthen a national or nationalistic identity.[1] There are always issues of self-involvement when studying human communities, past and present. The co-existence of insider and outsider perspectives is typical of the humanities.

Theology, in name the study of God but with greater metaphysical modesty perhaps better understood as the self-reflection of believers on their own heritage and stance in life, fits less easily among the humanities. In an essay on "The Conflict of the Faculties," in 1798, Immanuel Kant offered a view of the universities of his time, which consisted of three "higher faculties" that were to serve major professions, theology, law and medicine, and one "lower faculty," liberal arts or natural philosophy, covering what we now consider the sciences and humanities. The latter would be guided only by the quest for truth, whereas the higher faculties serve three major aims of the government in serving its people:

> first comes the *eternal* well-being of each, then his *civil* well-being as a member of society, and finally, his *physical* well-being (a long life and health). By public teachings about the *first* of these, the government can exercise very great influence to uncover the inmost thoughts and guide the most secret intentions of its subjects. By teachings regarding the *second*, it helps to keep their external conduct under the reins of public laws, and by its teachings regarding the *third*, to make sure that it will have a strong and numerous people to serve its purposes.[2]

1 Mary Fulbrook, *Historical Theory* (London: Routledge, 2002).

2 Immanuel Kant, "The Conflict of the Faculties," translated by Mary J. Gregor and Robert Anchor, in Immanuel Kant, *Religion and Rational Theology*, edited by Allen W. Wood and George di Giovanni (Cambridge University Press, 1996), 239–327, p. 250.

Professional schools such as Law, Medicine, Engineering, and Business, are part of major universities today. The faculty members of these schools may understand themselves in academic terms, but the professions for which they prepare their students are primarily important for their contributions to healthy and prosperous societies. In business and engineering, to give one example, "innovation" is not an academic ambition but one to be understood in the context of commercial progress.

Theology, too, is among the disciplines that train for a profession, ministry in a religious community. In the course of the eighteenth century, and even more in the nineteenth, in Europe and North America, various states came to define themselves as religiously neutral, in practice mostly merely neutral with respect to the variety of major Christian denominations. In some state universities, the academic discipline of theology was redefined in more neutral terms, as religious studies. The discipline of theology thereby descended from its position as the highest of the higher faculties into the sphere of the humanities, taking its place among the lower faculties. However, in the process ecclesiastical and personal interests did not disappear completely. The ways in which theology and religious studies are envisaged in relation to the modern university will offer us a window on the self-involving character of the humanities.

Before turning toward theology and religious studies, we will pay attention to philosophy. Philosophy seems to be better off, as it aspires to understand universal features of knowledge and reality, rather than being associated with sectarian identities and interests. If I analyze an argument philosophically, and consider it to be valid, this validity is a reasonable claim on my own position. It would be against the rational ethos of philosophy to accept a moral or epistemic argument as valid while based upon assumptions one accepts, without also accepting its conclusions. Philosophy thus fits well the legacy of the Enlightenment.

AIMING FOR UNIVERSALITY

Let us first consider how modern philosophy reflects key ideas from the European Enlightenment. At the end of his *Critique of Practical Reason*, originally from 1788, Immanuel Kant wrote of two awe-inspiring themes: Our knowledge of nature and our awareness of moral obligations.[3] Those lines have been inscribed on his grave in Königsberg, now Kaliningrad.

> Two things fill the mind with ever new and increasing admiration and reverence, the more often and more steadily one reflects on them: *the starry heavens above me and the moral law within me.*

The starry heavens: The natural world about which we have been able to discover so much. We discovered laws of nature, regularities that are the same everywhere and for everyone, whether one is in Japan, in Europe, in Africa, or even on the Moon. The sciences are a great model of universality and of cross-cultural collaboration and comprehension. The moral law within me: The basis for our duties, located in the person but also reasonable and hence valid for all.

Modern aspirations include knowledge and moral values that are universal. The natural sciences, dealing with "the starry heavens above," are an extremely successful global phenomenon. Moral claims articulated as universal human rights have been attractive in their global appeal, though in practice, we have fallen short of their ambitions, at first with respect to the position of women and of slaves, and in our time still too often with respect to persons of non-European descent. Nonetheless, I consider universal aspirations with respect to knowledge and morality indicative of deep values. The passage cited speaks of the heavens above and the moral law within. In the spirit of Kant's philosophy, one should also reflect upon, and come to admire in doing so, the *subject*, the person who seeks such knowledge of the world out there, who discerns such moral claims, who makes judgments.

The emphasis on universality does not work equally well in all domains of life. The dream of a universal language such as Esperanto, a language that would not be the language of any particular culture, failed, and so have visions for a world government and the desire to create a religion of humanity acceptable to all. Rightly so; some ambitions are too minimalist to live by. Humans are diverse in their ways of living, and this diversity is to be appreciated.

3 Immanuel Kant, *Practical Philosophy* (Cambridge University Press, 1996), p. 269.

The Enlightenment involved a critical attitude toward traditional sources of moral and epistemic authority, whether the Church, the King, or the Tradition. In an opinion piece on the question "What is Enlightenment?" Kant gave as the motto of the Enlightenment: "*Sapere aude*! Have the courage to make use of your own intellect!"[4] Modernity brought with it a conviction about the *autonomy* of the individual. Not as individualism, as if people should not care about family, friends, neighbors and others, or about social and political institutions; as humans we live and work with others. The autonomy is conceptual; one should make up one's own mind, rather than follow blindly the authority of a given community or tradition. A modern orientation rooted in the European Enlightenment combines universal ambitions, about knowledge and morality, with respect for individual autonomy and diversity.

We humans make judgments. "This is a good argument." "That is what we should do." "This is ugly." Judgments may be related to actions: If this is what we think we should do, we should do it. Other judgments are about the way we experience the world. That we find a sunset beautiful need not relate to action, except by inviting us to sit down and enjoy the moment. Aesthetic judgments are different from moral judgments, which seek to be univocal and universal. Aesthetic judgment with its flexibility and playfulness helps us see ourselves as people who make judgments and hence experience the world. By the use of imagination, we envisage possible ways of being in the world. I can envisage what I would do if I were in your position. We can imagine future generations, and thus come to see ourselves as part of humanity across generations. Imagination, creativity, aesthetic judgments: They give subjects the possibility to develop their capacity for self-reflection and envisaging a grander perspective, and with that develop as well their capacity for prudential and moral judgment.[5]

4 Kant, "An Answer to the Question: What Is Enlightenment?" in Kant, *Toward Perpetual Peace and Other Writings on Politics, Peace, and History* (New Haven, CT: Yale University Press, 2006), p. 17.

5 Dascha Düring and Marcus Düwell, "Towards a Kantian Theory of Judgment: The Power of Judgment in its Practical and Aesthetic Employment." *Ethical Theory and Moral Practice* 18 (2015), 943–956.

For judgments, there is always someone whose judgment it is. I experience a beautiful sunset. Given my aims, I hold this course of action necessary. Also, the moral judgment I make, implies a claim on myself; I have to live up to it. What is sketched here very briefly, is the turn to the subject that has characterized philosophy since the later work of Immanuel Kant. When we think about human knowledge, we have to think about the person who uses concepts and thereby constructs knowledge. When we think about moral and aesthetic judgments, we must envisage the person who makes such judgments.

With judgments might come self-reflection: Why do I think so? What do I value most? In a historical study or cultural analysis, we may seek to describe, explain, and understand judgments others make, the way they experience and understand the world. Perhaps their way of life remains strange to us; perhaps their ideas are in our opinion mistaken. But in philosophy, we also consider the *justification* of judgments, our own and those of others. What do I hold to be true or right? How should we live our lives? This is not merely about description; judgments become normative, prescriptive. Describing, explaining, and perhaps even understanding others need not involve such a commitment. "Justification" could be considered a third category, alongside explaining and understanding, Dilthey's *Erklären* and *Verstehen*, even though some, including Dilthey himself, include normative evaluation in the broader category of "understanding."

Philosophy is about thinking through questions, concepts, and arguments, and hence, seeking clarity by careful, systematic reflection. Doing philosophy is to be distinguished from studying the history of philosophy or the study of great philosophers. That might still be the study of ideas of others, of the same kind as the study of historical documents. Earlier thinkers may well be of use to help one develop clarity about questions and approaches; one can always learn from others. But studying those as persons who lived at a different time and in another context, is merely a stepping stone to address the question whether we consider their ideas justified, valid for us as well.

Doing philosophy is not writing a mission statement or positing a grand view. Nor should the question about one's philosophy be treated as similar to the question what my preferred music is. Someone who prefers classical music may have no reservations when learning that someone else prefers jazz. But someone who makes different judgments on truth or fairness than I do, thereby poses to me a challenge: Why do I disagree? Why do I consider those judgments mistaken? Such disagreements drive philosophy. If we have different views, who is right? If we speak different languages, we may have a practical problem, but I do not consider others mistaken for not speaking Dutch. Some differences are more troubling, as we would like to agree on moral values and on our understanding of the world.

Within the humanities there is a place for philosophy, for reflections that are argumentative, that seek to establish which judgments may be justified, and on which issues we can be pluralist without desiring arguments to justify choosing one position over another. In the first chapter, I offered a provisional definition of the humanities: Humanities are academic disciplines seeking understanding of human self-understandings and self-expressions, and of the ways in which people thereby construct their world. Philosophy offers a qualification of the understanding that is sought. It is not merely explanation, seeking to understand how certain humans came to construct their world in a particular way. Nor is it about understanding in the interpersonal sense, understanding what drives others. The important contribution to the humanities made by philosophy, is to evaluate convictions and practices. Also, in the process, to evaluate our processes of evaluation: What are the criteria and methods that are conducive of truth, or help us avoid error? What is fair, and what does it mean to be fair? Thus, we seek understanding and justification of the way we understand ourselves, our fellow humans, and our shared world.

Not all that is important is universal. A person, a piece of music, or some pursuit, may be important to me. This raises the question whether *particular* preferences can also serve as good reasons for the choices we make. How to think philosophically about reasons of love and the diversity of human identities?

REASONS OF LOVE AND THE WEALTH OF IDENTITIES

Moral judgments aspire to be universal, equally valid for all reasonable people. One may be tempted to grant universal values priority over personal concerns. But if moral values always take precedence over other values, there is no end in sight to the moral demand upon us. In a world that still has poverty and injustice, it would be inappropriate to invest any time and energy in creating art, making music, engaging in sports, reading novels, or writing books. "Moral saints," in the analysis of philosopher Susan Wolf, are missing out on much that makes life interesting.[6]

I want to have my dinner tonight; I am driven by selfish motives. Also, I am convinced of the moral importance of human rights, for all humans, whether I like them or not. However, I care existentially about my friends, my wife, my children, and grandchildren. Susan Wolf adds "reasons of love" alongside reasons that would qualify either as selfish or moral.[7]

> When I visit my brother in the hospital, or help my friend move, or stay up all night sewing my daughter a Halloween costume, I act neither for egoistic reasons not for moral ones. (. . .) I act neither out of self-interest nor out of duty or any sort of impersonal or impartial reason. Rather, I act out of love.

My relation to some specific persons is important to who I am, even when it would be accidental that my life has become interwoven with precisely these fellow humans.

So, too, for certain pursuits, that are important to me, pursuits that make me who I am, as a person, a subject and actor. Also, for my identity, the language that happens to be my own, the stories that inspire me, the way I celebrate and the way I mourn, the way I relate to my family, and the legacy I received. Such "loves" and other markers of identity are my particular way of being in the world. I never speak language; it is always a particular language. Adherents of a religion do not believe in religion; they are involved in particular rituals and stories; they participate in a community and its music. We have to balance two contrasting interests: universal ambitions, in knowledge

6 Susan Wolf, *The Variety of Values: Essays on Morality, Meaning, and Love* (Oxford University Press, 2015) includes her essay "Moral Saints," orig. *Journal of Philosophy* 79 (1982), 419–439.

7 Susan Wolf, *Meaning in Life and Why It Matters* (Princeton University Press, 2010), p. 4.

and morality, and a recognition of the worthwhile plurality of particular identities and loves.

The humanities mostly study particulars such as historical epochs, cultural practices, languages and dialects, authors, religious traditions, and much else. These are the material of human identities. Identities, whether religiously articulated, defined by citizenship, skin color, political preferences, family relationships, or other features, can be considered human constructions. This does not deny their reality, as constructions can be very real. Our whole world is full of human constructions, such as cities and computers. Social life is shaped by constructions, such as money and the state. Technology and culture are two major spheres of life that are constructions, and as such they are very real. Science is a human construction as well, one tested against the world, in a way that makes it the best model for knowledge that is as objective as possible. Human rights are constructions too, but as such they might be our best hope for a world in which all humans are treated fairly.

Identities are constructions. The philosopher Kwame Anthony Appiah gave a book on identities the title *The Lies That Bind: Rethinking Identity*.[8] Identities relate to our understanding of reality and to our values, but also to the heritage that formed us, the repertoire of stories that we use to educate and motivate, the music that moves us, the language, rituals and symbols we might use, the ways in which we dress ourselves. The identities we ascribe to others shape the ways we approach them, the assumptions we bring with us when we encounter them. Thus, identities are about the question with whom we identify, and with whom we are identified. Identities are individual but also communal; they may be religious or secular; they may be historically definite or fluid. They may appear to be naturally given, as gender and race, or defined politically or socially, as nationality and class. As human identities, they all may be contested and shown to be naive, also those initially treated as "naturally given." We have become aware of the social character of the simple binary assumption of two genders, male and female. Even at the biological level, it is not as simple as it may seem, and the social and cultural expectations

8 Kwame Anthony Appiah, *The Lies That Bind: Rethinking Identity* (London: Profile Books, 2018).

associated with the distinction between men and women are clearly those of humans, rather than being unavoidably facets of reality. Identities need not be *lies*, as Appiah's title provocatively states, but they aren't objective truth either.

Each of us has multiple identities, as humanity can be divided in various ways – by nationality, by gender, by age, by musical preference, and much else. Identities are labels, and with those labels come ideas about the people to whom a particular label does apply and to whom it does not. It includes and it excludes. An identity provides reasons; as a Hindu, one might prefer not to eat meat; as a Jew, pork will be excluded. Identities affect how others treat you; often with solidarity by those who belong "to the same group," sometimes exclusion by those who have a different identity.

We humans have habits, passions and convictions, a particular identity or even more than one. Also, if we consider ourselves not to be overly committed to a particular identity, we might be committed to a liberal, open-minded attitude; that then would be an element of who we are. We cannot have a "view from nowhere," to draw on a book title from Thomas Nagel, but always live with a view from now and here.[9] For me, that involves an academic identity, but also a European one, more specific a Dutch one, as well as my identity in family history, as a son and grandson, a husband, a father, and a grandfather.

Religion is an interesting example of identity. We, humans, care about causes that are dear to us; some might even consider some such causes sacred. We have beliefs about the world and our place in it, and engage in particular practices and rituals. Wearing a head scarf, celebrating Christmas, or practicing mindfulness: Our behavior signals who we are and the culture or subculture we belong to. Even "spirituals" and "nones" might be considered religious, though not identifying with a church or other religious institution. Atheists have their convictions and values too, about the non-existence of God and the irrelevance of worship.

For my understanding of identities, I borrow from the way Clifford Geertz understood religions. He wrote, some fifty years ago, that

9 Thomas Nagel, *The View from Nowhere* (Oxford University Press, 1986).

"sacred symbols function to synthesize a people's ethos – the tone, character, and quality of their life, its aesthetic style and mood – and their world view – the picture they have of the way things in sheer actuality are, their most comprehensive ideas of order." In a definition of "a religion" Clifford Geertz offered in the same essay, the combination of ethos and worldview returns as the distinction between "moods and motivations" and "a conception of a general order of existence"[10]:

> a religion is (1) a system of symbols which acts to (2) establish powerful moods and motivations in men by (3) formulating conceptions of a general order of existence and (4) clothing these conceptions with such an aura of factuality that (5) the moods and motivations seem uniquely realistic.

As an anthropologist, Geertz clearly looked at groups and their systems of symbols and structures of authority. We may be more individualistic, though identities, including religious labels, are again and again classifying people as members of a group. His definition may be too much about symbols and beliefs; there is also practice, habit, as emphasized by Appiah: "Habitus and identity are connected by the fact that we recognize certain forms of behaviour – accents, but also ways of walking, styles of dress – as the signs of certain forms of identity and that our identities shape our habitus unconsciously." Identities are labels assigned to people; not characteristics that all members of a particular group have, and will have forever. They are not fixed. It is as with other legacies we have received: "Our ancestors are powerful, though not in the ways the fundamentalists imagine. For none of us creates the world we inhabit from scratch; none of us crafts our values and commitments save in dialogue with the past."[11] With such caveats, about the importance of practice and the dynamic character of traditions, Geertz's definition about religions as systems of symbols brings together many elements that might be taken to characterize one's identity: The way one experiences the world and

10 Clifford Geertz, "Religion as a Cultural System," in M. Banton (ed.), *Anthropological Approaches to the Study of Religion* (London: Tavistock, 1966), 1–46, pp. 3 and 4; reprinted in Geertz, *The Interpretation of Cultures* (New York: Basic Books, 1973), 87–125, pp. 89 and 90.

11 Appiah, *The Lies That Bind*, pp. 25 and 67.

the way one believes one should act, and these have some permanence as the ways of experiencing the world and acting, the moods and motivations, are taken to be rooted in the way things are, their factuality.

The study of religion is an interesting cluster of disciplines. It started as "theology," one of the higher faculties, but has moved more and more into the domain of the humanities. The place of theology in the modern university thus provides an interesting window on the humanities, as it deals with the particularities and, for adherents, normative character of religious and non-religious identities, and the appropriateness of such studies in the modern academic climate.

THEOLOGY IN THE UNIVERSITY

Studying identities of others may be done professionally by listening and observing, while shelving one's own preferences. Such non-committal listening as an anthropological stance deviates significantly from normal social interaction. May we allow ourselves to engage as well in scholarship that involves our own identity more openly? The contemporary study of religion exemplifies the dual character of the humanities: studying human practices as social and cultural phenomena *and* studying religions for their potential meaning to ourselves in relation to others. In the remainder of this chapter we will consider *theology*, a discipline that has such partisan and personal characteristics, and its partial transformation into historical and philosophical studies of religion.

Must the study of religion always be the business of insiders, of theologians? Is it possible to understand religion without being religious? In his study *Das Heilige* (1917) Rudolf Otto wrote: "The reader is invited to direct his mind to a moment of deeply-felt religious experience, as little as possible qualified by other forms of consciousness. Whoever cannot do this, whoever knows no such moments in his experience, is requested to read no farther."[12] As an analogy, one might

12 Rudolf Otto, *The Idea of the Holy: An Inquiry into the Non-rational Factor in the Idea of the Divine and Its Relation to the Rational* (Oxford University Press, 1950), p. 8.

wonder whether someone who is tone deaf, could study music. According to Otto, personal experience is necessary to access the real meaning of religion.

However, just as with music, a historical and cultural study that does not assume experiential participation, is no doubt possible. Believers, insiders, are the authority on their own experiences and beliefs, but others may study those practices and beliefs in terms that suit their scholarship. The scholarly study of religion seeks knowledge about human beliefs and practices, as historical traditions and as lived religion. Knowledge that is as objective as possible by taking an "outsider perspective," that is, by suspending our own personal preferences and beliefs.

But still, such studies have a personal dimension. In theology, and in most of the humanities, we need to assume the others to be subjects who experience the world as meaningful, or perhaps as fragile, or even as a frightening abyss devoid of meaning. We assume them to be actors who act for reasons. We treat them as persons who seek to interpret their place in the social and cultural world and in the cosmos, who try to grasp their origins and think about their destiny. The scholar has to recognize the importance of a first-person perspective as a way of being in the world. However, the scholar need not share beliefs about God or the meaning of existence. How has the ensuing tension between normative theology and the agnostic orientation of humanities scholarship worked out for the position of theology in modern universities?

For most of human history, intellectual reflection upon beliefs and practices was the business of theologians, professionals within a community of faith. Theology, the intellectual articulation of beliefs and practices, served the education of children and converts, *catechesis*. It was also essential when theological disputes erupted, to decide who belongs to the community, what is to be rejected as heretical, and who should be expelled. As articulation of the self-understanding of communities, theologies served the authority and power of some, and excluded others.

In Europe's oldest universities, we find the distinction between four faculties: Theology, Law, and Medicine as the three higher faculties with a professional focus, and the *artes liberales*. The last one provided linguistic knowledge and skills, such as grammar (Latin), rhetoric, and dialectic (logic, reasoning), and knowledge with a mathematical orientation, arithmetic, geometry, musicology, and astronomy. Such a division of disciplines continued in universities in regions shaped by the European Reformation. As the University in Louvain, in Belgium, was in an area under Spanish Habsburg control, Protestants in the United Provinces in the northern part of the Low Countries needed their own university. Hence, the establishment of Leiden University, in 1575. In the initial procession there were four symbolic figures: *Sacra Scriptura, Justitia*, *Medicina*, and *Minerva*, who represented the faculties of theology, law, medicine, and the liberal arts.[13] Theology served to provide intellectual and ideological leadership, in particular for the Reformed, Calvinist, variety of Protestantism that characterized the Dutch Revolt against the Catholic Spanish. Training ministers for the Dutch churches was at least as important as teaching law and medicine.

In the nineteenth century, we see a professionalization of humanities, alongside the rise of the natural sciences. Characteristic for the period are the Enlightenment's resistance to traditional authorities, the Romantic interest in the local and unique, and a changing social and political landscape, including the demand for well-prepared teachers in an expanding realm of secondary and higher education. By the middle of the nineteenth century there had been various challenges to the established order; the *Communist Manifest* of 1848, of the emerging labor movement, is just one example. In 1848 in the Netherlands, King William II gave in to pressure for a more democratic constitution. Aspirations about the religious neutrality of the state has been an important facet in such developments. In France with its concept of *laicité*, it gave rise to an explicit exclusion of religious symbols from the public sphere. In the Netherlands, neutrality became understood in terms of equal treatment of recognized churches and religions.

Some schools of theology at distinguished American universities such as Harvard, Yale, Chicago, and Duke in the USA continue to carry the name "Divinity School," as do the faculties at Cambridge and

13 Willem Otterspeer, *The Bastion of Liberty: Leiden University Today and Yesterday* (Leiden University Press, 2008), p. 23.

Edinburgh, United Kingdom. Such a name suggests that their academic work deals with the divine, that is, with God, whereas in other schools we deal with human, social and natural realities. In Dutch, the traditional term for theology was *Godgeleerdheid*, which would translate as "learnedness about God." The Faculty of Law carries a similar name, *Rechtsgeleerdheid*, learnedness about law. Schools of Law and Divinity certainly are home to scholarship, learned, and erudite, perhaps one may even find a whiff of wisdom. One might wonder, however, whether the terms "divinity" or "theology" resonate with the modern idea of research, as it characterizes the humanities.

In the Netherlands, increased emphasis on the religious neutrality of the state found expression in two different arrangements for academic theological training, a *duplex ordo* model and a *simplex ordo* one. The *duplex ordo* model arose in 1876 with a new law on higher education. In general, higher education served to prepare for independent research and for professions that required academic education. At that time, the existence of a separate Faculty of Theology was in dispute, given the desire to separate state and church. Is the preparation of students for ministry an appropriate role for a public university? And if so, would a confessional program – with theology being understood as the science of God – be in line with academic standards? For some, the recognition of a personal, living God is the *sine qua non* for Theology. As this was not deemed acceptable in public universities, theology was almost pushed out of the Dutch universities. The construction that maintained a place for theology in the public universities in the Netherlands was a separation of roles, a *duplex ordo*, a twofold order. [14]

Dutch universities had been aligned with the established Reformed Church. Upon the model introduced in 1876 the government would appoint professors in the university, and these were supposed to treat their disciplines in a non-confessional way. "Church history" became

14 Otto de Jong, "De Wetgever van 1876 en de Theologie," *Nederlands Archief voor Kerkgeschiedenis*, Nieuwe serie, 48 (1968), 313–332. Faith as *conditio sine qua non*: Aart De Groot, "Geschiedenis van de Faculteit der godgeleerdheid aan de Utrechtse universiteit," in A. de Groot and O.J. de Jong (eds.), *Vier eeuwen Theologie in Utrecht: Bijdragen tot de Geschiedenis van de Theologische Faculteit aan de Universiteit Utrecht* (Zoetermeer: Meinema, 2001), 10–97, p. 48.

the history of Christianity, as a focus within historical studies. Biblical studies became the study of the texts, beliefs, and practices of people long ago, rather than a discipline that imported theological assumptions by reading the Old Testament in the light of the New Testament. Other subjects set in the law included the history of the doctrine of God, the history of religions in general, philosophy of religion, and ethics. Methodologically, theology in the public university moved closer to the humanities, though it remained a separate faculty.

Students who aspired to become ministers in the Dutch Reformed Church would supplement their undergraduate program with further studies in systematic and practical theology. This would be a distinct, separate stage in their training; hence, a *duplex ordo*. This additional program was taught by professors selected by the Reformed Church, though paid for by the state. These professors would not be professors *of* the university but professors *with* the university. This law made it possible to grant other Christian denominations a similar arrangement. Lutherans, Mennonites, and the Remonstrant Brotherhood, three Protestant denominations that had their roots in the sixteenth and seventeenth century, could appoint their own church professors and have their own supplementary programs at public universities. As these other Protestants expected similar skills and knowledge, e.g. requiring students to learn to read texts in Hebrew and Greek, it fitted well that they would use the same basic disciplines as taught by the university.

Whereas the *duplex ordo* characterized the public, state-funded universities, in 1880 a Calvinist group that broke away from the Reformed Church opened its own private university, the Vrije Universiteit (VU) in Amsterdam, free from the state *and* free from the national Reformed Church, which they considered too permissive of modernism. Abraham Kuyper, the founding father of the Free University, had converted to a strong Calvinist stance, with emphasis on human sin, divine grace, and ecclesial sovereignty. Under his leadership, this orientation was to find expression in the new university, most of all in its faculties of theology and philosophy. This structure came to be called *simplex ordo*. Within such a unified frame, all scholars faced academic *and* confessional expectations. Along similar lines, in the early twentieth century Catholics in the Netherlands established their own university in Nijmegen, now the Radboud

University, and a business school, now Tilburg University. In the course of the twentieth century the VU, the Catholic University in Nijmegen, and Tilburg University with its School of Catholic Theology, received full recognition by the government and public funding, on equal footing with the public universities in the Netherlands. In 1989, a Humanist university was recognized, serving secular and religious humanists, as humanist counselors in the military, in prisons and in hospitals had come to serve alongside chaplains, imams, rabbis, pandits, and others. Thus, the Netherlands developed a pluralist model of religious neutrality, which matched for most of the twentieth century a "pillarized" social landscape of co-existing communities.

Elsewhere in Europe, other arrangements for the religious neutrality of the state arose. In Germany, one finds in parallel Catholic and Evangelical theological faculties. ("Evangelisch" refers to the Lutheran and Reformed forms of Christianity in Germany; it is not to be identified with "evangelical" in the sense of Anglo-Saxon branches of Christianity with emphasis on personal conversion.)

In his address as rector of Berlin University in 1901, titled *Die Aufgabe der theologischen Fakultäten und die allgemeine Religionsgeschichte,* on the task of the theological faculties and general history of religions, the theologian Adolf Harnack held up the developments in Netherlands as a bad example. Transforming a faculty of Christian theology into one of religious studies is not a good idea, as for each religion one needs to study the relevant language and historical context; studying all religions is simply asking too much, and thus would result in amateurism. Besides, the texts and languages of various traditions are already studied in faculties of arts and languages. Most remarkable as an argument I find the following: To understand religion, it would be sufficient to focus on Christianity, a tradition with the Bible, a history of almost three thousand years, and available today as a living tradition. "*Wer diese Religion nicht kennt, kennt keine, und wer sie sammt ihre Geschichte kennt, kennt alle*" – Whoever does not know Christianity, knows none; who knows Christianity and its history, knows all. Having the Bible, one can understand other traditions that claim to possess holy books. Christianity encompasses pure monotheism as well as something more akin to polytheism, in the

Roman Catholic adoration of saints. Last but not least, Christianity is not *a* religion among many, but rather "*the* religion." The Bible and Jesus Christ should be considered the center of all theological studies.[15]

Germany today continues to have schools of theology, both Protestant and Roman Catholic, at major universities. More recently some chairs in Islamic theology, especially to serve the training of secondary school teachers, have been created. The focus on distinct faculties for Protestantism and Catholicism might reflect as well the hermeneutical emphasis that arose in the first half of the nineteenth century. As Friedrich Schleiermacher, professor of theology at the university in Berlin, approached the topic, theology is not to be understood as a scholarly discipline that engages in metaphysical-theological discourse, about God. God might be beyond the reach of academic scholarship. Instead, theology focuses on the self-understanding of Christian communities. In his main exposition, *The Christian Faith*, originally from 1821–1822, he offers 172 theses, each with a substantial explication. Early in his exposition, he emphasizes that the referent of theology is the Christian church, and particular the piety that is at the heart of the community, a piety that is "neither a Knowing nor a Doing, but a modification of Feeling, or of immediate self-consciousness." The common element in all expressions of piety, is the consciousness of ourselves "as absolutely dependent, or, which intends the same meaning, as being in relation with God." Thus, systematic theology serves the community by thinking through the fundamental life-orientation of the believers.[16] Or, in a more secular setting, by offering ways to understand our human existence. In the process, it is also self-reflective, about the position assumed by the theologian and by the experiencing religious person in general. In terms that go back to Kant, it could also be seen as focusing on the conditions for the subject of religious experiences and understanding.

Such a self-understanding of theology is not unusual today. It can be considered a "hermeneutical turn," as it focuses primarily on the

15 Adolf Harnack, *Die Aufgabe der theologischen Fakultäten und die allgemeine Religionsgeschichte* (Giessen: Ricker's Verlagsbuchhandlung, 1901), p. 11.

16 Friedrich Schleiermacher, *Christian Faith, Volume One* (Louisville, KY: Westminster John Knox, 2016); quotes from theses 3 and 4.

people, the way they interpret their own tradition and their lives in the light of that tradition. Unlike historical or sociological studies, it is existentially loaded, as it involves the question what the tradition might mean to us today. However, it avoids the focus on speculative metaphysical issues that could lead to the exclusion of theology from the university. A hermeneutical theology is about personal orientation, informed by knowledge of the texts and history of the tradition. Such a transformation of theology brings these faculties more in line with modern schools of humanities than theology before the nineteenth century was. However, with the focus on a particular confessional community, it is more like the *simplex ordo* institutions mentioned above than seems suitable for a school of humanities as such. Similar issues regard seminaries and Christian Colleges in the United States, as these often have a confessional background. Their underlying commitments may show up in governance, in the palette of courses taught, and in appointments and programs in theology and philosophy.

In recent years, in the Netherlands the term *Godgeleerdheid* and its equivalent, theology, has almost completely disappeared as the name for a school in research universities in the Netherlands. Theology is often regarded as too metaphysical, reaching beyond what can be studied empirically and historically. And at the same time as too parochial, as referring only to Christianity. Most importantly, by speaking of theology, the approach seems bound to a different type of authority, that of a church. In public universities in the Netherlands, what remains of the study of religion now mostly has its place within schools of humanities.

Returning to the Dutch Higher Education Law of 1876: In relation to new institutional arrangements that reflected a greater emphasis on the religious neutrality of the state, Dutch public universities recognized two new disciplines: The History of Religions, as comparative religious studies was called then, and Philosophy of Religion, as the non-dogmatic version of systematic theology. "History of Religions" sounds academically neutral, but the study of myths and images of other people often was associated with a liberal religious agenda. Philosophy of Religion was the most theological of the disciplines allowed within a public university, focusing more on rational argument than on affectively appealing stories. We will consider the creation of these two new disciplines, to illuminate ways in which personal engagement and self-reflection may be present within the humanities.

CASE STUDY (1): HISTORY OF RELIGIONS AS A NEW DISCIPLINE

Theology used to be Christian theology. Religions such as Islam and Hinduism were mostly treated in schools of languages or arts. Sometimes also in law schools; Leiden University trained civil servants for the Dutch East Indies, now Indonesia, and these future civil servants needed competence in local legal and cultural traditions shaped by Islam and Hinduism. The study of religions other than Christianity was primarily functional, but with the new Law on Higher Education of 1876, the study of religions other than Christianity became a legitimate subject within schools of theology at public universities in the Netherlands.

Cornelis Petrus Tiele (1830–1902), a specialist on religions of antiquity such as Zoroastrianism, was the first professor of the History of Religions, at Leiden University. The other founding father of the discipline, which could also have been named Science of Religions, was Friedrich Max Müller, introduced in the previous chapter as the driving force behind the book series *Sacred Books of the East*. Tiele had been a minister in the Remonstrant Brotherhood, one of the smaller Protestant Churches, and as of 1873 had come to serve as the director of the Remonstrant Seminary at Leiden, by then modernist in orientation. His subsequent chair in the history of religions had its place within a faculty that still had the name Theology, and which continued to serve as the first stage in the training of Protestant ministers. This combination of scholarship and a religious orientation fitted well with Tiele's liberal Protestantism and his interest in the history of religions.

Proponents of such a science of religion intended a radical transformation of theology into science of religion. From their view, the science of religion was not only descriptive, but also an evaluative discipline. It could fulfil most of the tasks of the old theology and in the process was expected to show the superiority of Christian religion or of a transformed version of Christianity. Tiele speculated about "a purified, liberal Protestantism developing into the religion of mankind, on the basis of a true, complete humaneness." Theology had been transformed into the history of religions, but at the same time, the history of religions had a theological, or at least a religious drive, though metaphysical questions are explicitly excluded; the object of study is human religion. But even then: "There is no reason, Tiele argued, to see the science of religion as a threat to religion, just as linguistics is not harmful to language." Learning other languages need not undermine love for one's mother tongue.[17]

The liberal–protestant inspiration of comparative religious studies did not go unchallenged. At the First International Congress for the History of Religions, in Paris in 1900, Müller and Tiele became honorary presidents of the congress, even though they both were absent. But many participating scholars also felt "that the comparative study of religion should no longer be regarded as the maidservant of liberal theology or an auxiliary to the search for a universal religion based on inter-religious dialogue," as Lourens Van den Bosch notes in his biography of Müller. At a later moment in the Dutch science of religion, in the 1970s, methodological agnosticism became the main approach with the work of Theo Van Baaren in Groningen. Still, in a more recent review article, Jan Platvoet discerns "poly-paradigmaticity," as within the faculties of theology religionist, reductionist, and agnostic approaches continue to exist side by side.[18]

A recent example of personal religious engagement with scholarship might be provided by considering an autobiographical book by Elaine Pagels, a Princeton expert on gnostic gospels and other early Christian literature that the Church had deemed heretical. Those texts had been lost for many centuries, but fragments were rediscovered in the twentieth century. In her book *Why Religion? A Personal Story*, she shows "how exploring the history of religion connects with experiences in my

17 Arie L. Molendijk, *The Emergence of the Science of Religion in the Netherlands* (Leiden: Brill, 2005), pp. 81 and 104.

18 Lourens P. van den Bosch, *Friedrich Max Müller: A Life Devoted to the Humanities* (Leiden: Brill, 2002), p. 514; Jan Platvoet, "Pillars, Pluralism and Secularisation: A Social History of Dutch Sciences of Religions," in G. Wiegers and J.G. Platvoet (eds.), *Modern Societies and the Science of Religions: Studies in Honor of Lammert Leertouwer* (Leiden: Brill, 2002), 82–148.

own life." When she entered graduate studies in religion at Harvard, she had left the unengaging main stream Christianity of her parental home as well as a more vivid evangelical engagement she had been involved in for some time. By then, she had become interested in the question how such movements began and what could be known about Jesus. To her, these were not merely academic questions; her studies were driven as well by a spiritual quest. She came across the gnostic gospels and other heretical writings of early Christianity. The seventieth saying attributed to Jesus in the *Gospel of Thomas* speaks to her: "*If you bring forth what is within you, what you will bring forth will save you. If you do not bring forth what is within you, what you do not bring forth will destroy you.*" Bringing forth "what is within you"; for her, religion is about the depth dimension in a person's life, rather than about a reality "out there."

Much later, confronted with creation stories from a people in Sudan, the Dinka, she rejects the treatment of creation stories as primitive science. "Instead, creation stories help create the *cultural* world, by transmitting traditional values." As the use of biblical references in disputes on homosexuality has shown, the Genesis "story still works as a cultural Rorschach test, to which countless people, religious or not, reflexively turn when they encounter something that makes them uncomfortable. For creation stories claim to tell how the world was *meant* to be, or how it *should* be – how it was in the beginning."[19]

As a modern person, she writes that she held that we do not *find* meaning; "The most we could hope was that we might be able to *create* meaning." However, while at a time of deep sorrow meditating with a Trappist, Roman Catholic monk, she experiences "waves of energy coming towards me from various directions," adding, "I was surprised, not having imagined that actual transactions might occur." Stories can be meaningful, even if one does not believe them to be true in a descriptive sense. We use stories: "For while scholars of literature like to say that we use stories to 'think with,' we also use them to 'feel with' – that is, to find words for what otherwise we could not say." Another example arises when she writes about ideas about Satan:

19 Elaine Pagels, *Why Religion? A Personal Story* (New York: HarperCollins, 2018), pp. xiv, 23, and 52.

"although I didn't *believe in* him, the figure often called "the old enemy" nevertheless lived in my imagination, shaped by ancient cultural traditions, catalyzed by crisis." She keeps the scholarly sense, of relating ideas to context, to social and cultural history, to *people* having ideas they articulate in this way, but those people include ourselves.

> In [the Gospel of] Thomas, then, the "good news" is not only about Jesus; it's also about every one of us. For while we ordinarily identify ourselves by specifying how we differ, in terms of gender, race, ethnicity, background, family name, this saying suggests that recognizing that we are "children of God" requires us to recognize how we are the same – members, so to speak, of the same family. These sayings suggest what later becomes a primary theme of Jewish mystical tradition: that the "image of God," divine light given in creation, is hidden deep within each one of us, linking our fragile, limited selves to their divine source.

When another scholar challenges her for reading her own experiences into those ancient texts, rather than studying these in their historical context, she responds that such historical scholarship, though important and valuable, offers only limited understanding. The engagement with the text is self-involving; "while I work on these sayings, they work on me." Such texts are not so much of interest for the doctrines involved, but as texts collected by people who sought to deepen their spiritual practice. Those stories show different ways of interpreting one's life, shaped by temperament and situation. They are "myth as Plato told it: imagination revealing the deeper truths of human experience."[20]

Her emphasis on stories is primarily affective, what they do to us in times of grief and guilt, and how they help us understand others, develop empathy. However, as she refers to Plato, usually considered a founding figure of philosophy, it may be appropriate to consider the other "new" discipline introduced with the 1876 law in the Netherlands, the Philosophy of Religion, which tends to focus more on rationality.

20 Pagels, *Why Religion?*, pp. 104, 129 (2x), 168, 146, 177, 178, 203.

CASE STUDY (2): PHILOSOPHY OF RELIGION

In the process of separating the public university's professorships and the church-related chairs, existential and normative issues that had been central to theology landed on the side of the church professors; such issues depended too much upon confessional orientations. However, on the public side, a new discipline was created, "philosophy of religion," which allowed for theological discussion without confessional constraints. My teacher in philosophy of religion at the University of Groningen, Hubertus G. Hubbeling, defined the task of philosophy of religion in relation to the science of religion, as the historical and anthropological study of religion, as follows:

> The question of the truth of religious statements is in my opinion the central problem of the philosophy of religion. Philosophy of religion distinguishes itself from science of religion precisely on this point. Science of religion does not ask for the truth or falseness of religious institutions or statements, it just describes and explains them. Philosophy of religion, then, may be characterized as follows:
> *Philosophy of religion = science of religion + the investigation of truth or falsity.*

In its interest in truth, philosophy of religion thus comes close to systematic theology, the intellectual concern of the insider. However, there is a distinction between a philosopher of religion and a systematic theologian:

> in a philosophical argument a reference to revelation is not permitted, whereas in theology one may refer to revelation as an argument.

Hence, in philosophy of religion scholars should not base their considerations on particular religious creeds, revelations, or experiences, but rather attempt to think through the truth and value *of* religion in light of the best available truth *about* religions.[21]

Within religious studies there is also a concern about truth, as scholars seek to come up with true knowledge about a tradition, its history, its texts, its practices, and so on, and they base their knowledge

21 H. G. Hubbeling, *Principles of the Philosophy of Religion* (Assen, NL: Van Gorcum, 1987), pp. 3 and 1. This section draws on Willem B. Drees, *Over wijsbegeerte van de godsdienst en haar object: Twee formules* (Universiteit Leiden, 2002).

claims upon research in the field and in archives. They may seek to understand what the religious stories might mean to those telling them. For instance, stories about "life after death" may have major consequences in this life, individually and socially, and making the impact of those stories visible is a task of religious studies. But upon this view, religious studies is *methodologically agnostic*. That is, scholars are not expected to discuss the question whether those beliefs are true, whether it is plausible to believe in life after death. Such a methodological agnosticism is typical of religious studies.

The philosopher of religion, as understood here, shares this agnostic attitude only to some extent, as a philosopher may enter into a discussion on the claims involved in those beliefs. In this sense, an outspoken atheist such as the Dutch philosopher Herman Philipse in his *God in the Age of Science?* acts as a philosopher of religion, arguing for a particular conclusion about the truth, or in his case rather the falsity or meaninglessness, of religious beliefs.[22] The philosopher, like the theologian, is interested professionally in the claims a religion makes, the truth of the religion, as distinct from historical truths about a religion.

One might distinguish three roles for such a philosopher of religion. One is conceptual analysis, considering the clarity and consistency of the concepts and ideas involved. This could also involve a logical reconstruction, how one might understand the ideas. A second task regards the engagement with empirical and historical knowledge. How do those ideas relate to what else we know about reality? Much work on "religion and the natural sciences," a field of discussion in which I have been involved, is of this kind. Also, third, a philosopher might ask questions not so much about the ideas themselves but rather about general issues. What do we mean by truth in this context? What might be suitable criteria? How might one know? What is the nature of religious language?

Some philosophies of religion have been liberal, playing with ideas as possible views of reality. They may be inclusivist, seeing similar motives and aims across traditions. Others have been apologetic, articulating arguments for the existence of God or for particular

22 Herman Philipse, *God in the Age of Science? A Critique of Religious Reason* (Oxford University Press, 2012).

theological doctrines. "Negative apologetic," arguing that atheistic critiques do not hold, has been quite common in philosophy of religion as articulated by self-declared "Christian" philosophers.[23]

Here, I would like to advocate that the philosopher of religion may be positioned as a *mediator* between empirically and historically oriented research, typical of religious studies, and the "insider perspective" of believers and theologians.

Such philosophical mediation is quite common. A scientist might speak of hormones whereas the subject claims to be in love, enchanted by a smile and personality. Humans speak of ideas, ideals and feelings, where a psychologist or sociologist might see interests and group pressure, while a neurologist measures brain activity. Even science, the study of nature, may be considered in a dual perspective, as a quest for truth, driven by rational considerations and experience, and as an all-too human social enterprise, historically contingent, driven by desires for power and reward. Philosophy might serve as mediator between such perspectives, by dispelling false oppositions such as the one between brain and mind, or the one between evolved and moral. The philosophy of mind is typically addressing the question how neural processes can be bearers of meaningful discourse. Meta-ethics and philosophy of biology concern the multiple ways in which evolutionary history might give rise to moral individuals. The philosophy of science is addressing the question how fallible human practices can deliver more or less objective, culture-independent knowledge.

Why would philosophy of religion be relevant? I am somewhat reluctant to appeal to "wisdom," to particularly deep insight. Rather, to assess what is reasonable in a world overwhelmed by emotions and interests is of utmost importance, especially in relation to religions. *Socially*, given the grip that religious authorities and communities may have over individuals, for good or evil. *Pastorally*, seeking reasonable truth is important, so that people are not fooled with pseudo-science, pseudo-religion, and pseudo-therapies, providing false hope for real money. One might even argue that *theologically* a philosophical

23 John Hick, *An Interpretation of Religion: Human Responses to the Transcendent* (Basingstoke: Macmillan, 1989); James F. Sennett (ed.), *The Analytic Theist: An Alvin Plantinga Reader* (Grand Rapids: Eerdmans, 1998).

approach is important, even if faith is claimed to deal with the irrational in our idea of God, to paraphrase Rudolf Otto's subtitle of *The Holy*, as faith should not be directed to a cheap mystery, a magic trick. Those who look for a mystery at the heart of it all, should allow for challenging questions, rather than exclude them. Only if one lets go of false protection and allows for rational analysis as far as it gets, can one honestly claim an open end, a mystery at the heart of reality, a transcendence beyond human existence, a Ground of Being underling our existence, or whatever one might suspect to lie beyond the knowable.

Not only in the West is philosophy a context for religious reflection. To a panel discussion on the controversy on Wendy Doniger's *The Hindus: An Alternative History*, discussed in the previous chapter, the Hindu scholar and practitioner Anantanand Rambachan offered a contribution, as an involved but reflective insider. He points out the particular historical context of negative responses to Western scholarship. A negative reception of Western scholarship may reflect a concern about academic inequality, ever since the colonial period. More relevant to our topic here, to him the tension between Hindu studies on Hinduism and Western scholarship on Hinduism also reflects a difference in disciplinary setting. In the Western academic context, Hinduism is studied with historical and social-scientific methods. That enriches the understanding of the tradition, "but gives less attention to the claim of the tradition to reveal important truths about the nature of reality that are essential for human well-being and to the evaluation and normative implications of such claims." In contrast, he writes: "In Indian universities, the scholarly study of religion occurs, in most cases, in departments of philosophy."[24] Thus, in such scholarship the focus is less on empirical diversity, but rather on the ideas themselves, considering normative questions, whether those of the dominant discourse or those of others, critical and explorative.

Though one may accept such a role for philosophical reflection, whether on Hinduism or Christianity, it seems too easy a way to avoid the challenges that a more pluralistic historical analysis might put on

24 Anantanand Rambachan, "Academy and Community: Overcoming Suspicion and Building Trust," *Journal of the American Academy of Religion* 84 (2016), 367–372, p. 371.

the table. As happened in the controversy referred to above, the tension also involves issues that are preliminary to the academic ideas themselves: *Which* ideas are considered? *Who* is supposed to speak for the tradition?

The modern condition is not only pluralist in the sphere of ideas. Convictions and insights may have practical consequences. Thus, a question is also how we should live with the diversity that is there. To what extent can the humanities offer helpful insights in a pluralist age?

LIVING WITH DIVERSITY

Our existence is tied up with others. We inherit language, culture, and technology from others; we share the world with our contemporaries. The social reality we live in is not homogeneous. One facet of our condition is diversity, or even super-diversity – not just a diversity of homogeneous groups, but diversity within such groups, a diversity of influences and labels on each individual, a multitude of diversities.

For the sake of simplicity, here I will limit myself to diversity, the co-existence of various groups within modern society, assuming each to have a clearly demarcated identity. Diversity, and awareness thereof, is enhanced by urbanization and globalization, facilitated by digitalization and worldwide communication. Again, I draw on my Dutch experience, where societal diversity is most visible in terms of groups that reflect the European expansion through trade and colonialism (e.g., with roots in Indonesia, the Dutch Antilles, and Surinam) and labor migration in the 1960s, mostly from Turkey and Morocco. How to deal with such plurality?

One of the ways I encountered this diversity, was by teaching in a program on world religions. In this program a substantial number of Muslim students participated, often second or third generation Dutch, descending from grandparents who had arrived from Morocco and Turkey. But the program also attracted students with an interest in Buddhism, Christianity, Judaism, Wicca (or nature religions), and spirituality, as well as students who considered themselves fully secular.

In the very first class I taught in this program, I discussed with freshman students their understanding of religion. Some students emphasized the social dimension: Religions are traditions that shape communities within which people care for each other and are inspired to love their neighbors. Others pointed out the orientation toward something higher, the divine. Love of the neighbor and of God: Two important facets of religion, both seen in a positive light.

That same day airplanes flew into the Twin Towers of the World Trade Center in New York. A week later, I met with the same students. They had become sensitive to the darker potential of religion. Socially: A community has boundaries; others are excluded. Also, with the focus on something higher, some believers may consider it legitimate to act upon the absolute truth they claim has been revealed to them. On September 11, 2001, we again saw the ambivalence of ways people draw on religion to legitimize their actions.

On November 2, 2004, during a coffee break, we learned that earlier that morning the film maker Theo van Gogh had been killed on the street in Amsterdam, by a Dutch Muslim. Van Gogh had written columns about Dutch Muslims, and he had directed *Submission*, a film that was highly critical of the treatment of women in Islam – as if he could speak for those women. Many Muslims found his film and columns offensive. One of the students in the class explained to the other students what the writings and films of Van Gogh had done to him and his friends, young Muslims in the Netherlands. His words evoked a strong response from other students, as if by his explanation he justified the murder. That was not what he did, nor was it what he intended. However, in tense times, people are suspicious, even of the attempt to understand motives and ideas of extremists. Again and again, we need to distinguish between explaining and justifying radical human choices.

In 2007 I spoke in a series titled "What brings us together." The organizers were concerned that religious and ethnic diversity would overwhelm us. They posed the question what we have in common, despite all our differences. The organizers offered as their hypothesis that shared origins or moral commonalities among religious and secular traditions outweigh moral differences.[25]

25 Willem B. Drees, "Religies in een pluriforme samenleving," in *Wat ons bindt* (Amsterdam: De Rode Hoed & VU Podium, 2008), 35–44.

I challenged their assumptions, though I share their desire for social harmony. The quest for shared roots seems to me academically and morally misguided. Having a shared origin is not sufficient to guarantee harmony, as shown by every fratricide, as witnessed by the biblical story of Cain and Abel, and proven again by every civil war. Nor is a shared origin in historic times necessary; it might exclude, among others, aboriginals in Australia, Native Americans, and the peoples of Papua New Guinea. The hope that religious studies can enhance mutual acceptance today by pointing out a shared origin, by relating the traditions at stake all to Abraham or to some other mythical time, is misguided.

Appeals to a common origin are not historically descriptive. Rather, they seek to offer a normative "creation story" in scholarly garb. When providing a story of common origins, the history of religions may inspire. If it works for those addressed thus, that may be a good thing. However, such a normative use of history has its dangers. It may exclude those who do not fit in the origin myth, such as the aboriginals just mentioned. Also, within the religions that are included in the story, it may exclude those considered too "orthodox," those who are not inclined to treat other religions as equally adequate ways to the same higher goal. A shared origin is neither necessary nor sufficient, as shown by civil wars and heresy trials. Appealing to a common story of the origin of religions may have more disadvantages than advantages.

Well-meaning people might think of a different way to argue for commonality despite differences. Have not all religions come to similar conclusions, the same recommendations for behavior? Are there not everywhere versions of the Golden Rule, the conviction that we should treat one's neighbor as one wants to be treated oneself?

Yes, one can find such similarities. Differences too. An expert in Japanese studies, William LaFleur, compared views on organ donation in the United States and Japan. In the USA, Christian churches have encouraged organ donation. The first heart transplant was in 1967. In the 1960s, *agapè*, a Greek word used for neighborly love, had become a central notion in the Christian ethos. A love that encompasses those one does not know, even one's enemies. Thus, such love was detached from *eros* and from *philia*, brotherly love. *Agapè* would be love that would be indifferent to emotions and personal relationships. The religious vocabulary at that time in the West thus was conducive to a positive attitude toward organ donation, even to total strangers. In contrast, in Japan, violating the body of a deceased family member was considered at odds with familial respect, and hence organ donation met with substantial resistance. Not that there is no notion of love for others, but in a different constellation of convictions, the way it worked out, was different. Such differences are not to be dismissed as "modern" versus "outdated." On both sides, they are appropriating traditions in modern ways.[26] With respect to religious traditions, one can argue that there are interesting moral similarities *and differences.*

If religions don't have enough in common to bring us together, should it not be time to do without religious identities? Or at least, restrict their role to the private sphere, excluding religious arguments as contributions to public deliberation? In a pluralistic society, they will not convince others anyhow. Thus, let us use a neutral discourse, of human rights and democratic deliberation.

Such a plea for neutral discourse in the public sphere, and a clear distinction of public and private, is too grandiose. Esperanto was an artificially created language that would be the shared language of all rather than the language of a particular country. Thus, it would contribute to world peace. It did not become the global second language. It was actively taught in Iran under Khomeini, perhaps to counter the dominance of English as a global language. Later, the government of Iran turned against Esperanto, as it was promoted by the Baha'i, a religious movement that appealed to a prophet who had lived much more recently than Muhammed. Esperanto's aspiration of neutrality was contested again and again. So, too, a moral Esperanto, a non-partisan way of discussing moral and political issues, will be open to challenges, as its claim to neutrality reflects a liberal or a technocratic orientation. Controversies will not only play out within that language, but also be about that language. A language that is rich enough to articulate moral convictions and underlying motives, cannot be a language that is perceived as neutral by all. A neutral language for moral discourse excludes many who consider themselves

26 William R. LaFleur, "From Agapè to Organs," *Zygon: Journal of Religion and Science* 37 (2002), 623–642.

to be orthodox, rooted in a tradition, who use its images, stories, texts, and instructions to articulate their values and feelings. Excluding reference to the Bible and other particular texts and traditions makes it hard for them to participate in an authentic way, as their way of expressing convictions is excluded. [27]

Assuming that we need a common neutral language suggests that in the social process we need to understand each other fully and come to agree. But living together is a practical challenge, not a theoretical one. We don't need a shared identity, but tolerance for diversity, patience, and procedures that allow us to come together in different majorities when decisions are needed, taking into consideration the concerns of those who think otherwise. Excluding particular identities, for instance by limiting social and political discourse to a neutral language, is not adequate to human nature. It also asks for more than is needed. Living together, including moral and political deliberation, can live well with arguments that are not shared, or even understood, by all. It asks for civility, patience, and procedures, not for agreement.

CONCLUDING COMMENTS

Theology started as a normative discipline, associated with a given religious tradition and its authorities. With the development of modern academic approaches, it transformed into the study of human practices and beliefs, of ancient texts and historical processes, and thus became one of the humanities. The humanities seek knowledge that is independent of the knower: facts about particulars, in history, in languages, and all-over human culture, and patterns across the diversity of contexts.

However, the humanities are also subject-involving, seeking to understand others and oneself. That shows in the history of religions, or comparative religious studies, and in philosophy of religion. In religious studies, one may engage the stories, myths, and practices of others, but these stories and practices may also become significant for

27 Paul Cliteur, *Moreel Esperanto: Naar een autonome ethiek* (Amsterdam: Arbeiderspers, 2007); see also his *The Secular Outlook: In Defense of Moral and Political Secularism* (Malden, MA: Wiley Blackwell, 2010). Critical of exclusion: Jeffrey Stout, *Democracy and Religion* (Princeton University Press, 2004).

the scholar or reader, as an opportunity to reflect upon oneself and one's own legacy and as a model to be followed. Stories and images may evoke empathy for others, and help oneself deal with anger, guilt, and other emotions. Scholarly speaking, there is a risk involved, of reading one's own ideas into the texts, rather than respecting the otherness of others; we should not be too naive about using other people's myths. Thus, systematic analysis, as in philosophy and hermeneutic theology, is also important.

If we see the humanities as academic disciplines seeking *understanding of human self-understandings and self-expressions, and of the ways in which people thereby construct their world*, the academic engagement with religion makes clear that understanding has two sides. One is a quest for knowledge, for understanding something that might be alien, and not necessarily of personal interest. However, understanding is also self-involving, as it relies upon the assumption that those others one seeks to understand are humans, subjects to whom the world is meaningful. Whether in the humanities we seek knowledge about others or seek to understand ourselves better, it is important that there is quality. That is what scholarship is about. That will be the focus of the next chapter, on responsible scholarship in the humanities.

4

Responsible Scholarship

We need objective knowledge, or at least, knowledge that is as reliable as possible, given human fallibility and gullibility. We ought to pursue such knowledge, as ideas and claims may inspire and inform actions, and thus their truth matters morally. But a scholar is human, with personal preferences, values, and biases. How to be a responsible scholar? As we seek to avoid bias due to personal preferences, the question becomes what kind of neutrality might be appropriate in the humanities. To what extent can we expect a scholar in the humanities to deliver knowledge that is value-free, or rather, knowledge that is guided by knowledge-promoting values? Concerns about bias arise in the humanities with force because those who are the object of studies, may claim their say on how they are portrayed. When knowledge is considered offensive, they might feel that they deserve more respect than a particular scholar has given them. How to deal with the personal dimension of research?

The natural sciences earn their credit by methodical research. Various branches of knowledge have their own tools and procedures, while also drawing on those of other disciplines. Those tools and procedures are in flux, as existing tools are refined and new ones are added, opening up new windows on reality. In the humanities, inventive scholars also use technological and computational tools; a recent example is the rise of "digital humanities," scholars using modern technologies to analyze big data sets, whether of texts, images, historical events, or cultural practices, comparatively and diachronically. Here, we will limit ourselves to a brief reflection on similarities and dissimilarities between humanities and the sciences, in the inductive and hypothetical-deductive development of knowledge. With that development of knowledge comes the fear of reduction, of claims that a rich phenomenon can be understood in terms that might not really do justice to the phenomenon. The natural sciences earn their credit also by their results, such as the development of general theories and the discovery of laws of nature such as Newton's law of gravity. To what extent is the discovery of patterns in the humanities similar to the discovery of natural laws? Before we discuss the role of the scholar and seek to learn from similarities and differences with the sciences, we begin with the basic human need for reliable knowledge.

FALLIBLE AND GULLIBLE HUMANS NEED RELIABLE KNOWLEDGE

We, humans, make mistakes. Our memories fall short. Our senses, our reasoning, and our language distort reality. We are misled easily, by prejudices, emotions, and group think. We may rationalize our interests and cover our mistakes. We embrace new information that supports our convictions, and we play down challenges. That is, we suffer from confirmation bias. Also, others may fool us, to our disadvantage. We cannot be sure about claims of others, and should not be too confident about our own observations. False claims to knowledge can damage people. Checks and double checks are necessary.

Understanding ourselves as limited and fallible is the basic human self-understanding that drives all of science and scholarship. There is an optimistic side to this self-understanding; we believe we can do better. If we make an effort, we expect to avoid some mistakes. With the sober assessment of human fallibility comes a high norm, out of love for fellow humans: we should aspire to avoid mistakes. This simple and humble task is as old as humanity, at least since humans made spikes in clay tablets as a solid check for fallible memories.

The philosopher Francis Bacon argued in 1620 in his *Novum Organum* that humans are prone to four types of misleading ideas, which he called *idols*: The *idols of the tribe*, inherent in human nature and the human mind, such as seeing patterns in a configuration of stars, the *idols of the cave*, reflecting an individual's perspective, temperament, education, habit and the like, the *idols of the market place*, as we may be misled by the language used in our social interactions, and the *idols of the theater*, as we may be misled by ideologies, philosophies, religions, and false learning. To counter the power of such idols, we should devote ourselves to careful observations and controlled experiments.[1]

Whereas Bacon expected that our prejudices can be overcome by empirical studies, the philosopher and mathematician René Descartes warned in 1641 that we can be misled by our senses as well. For all we know, the world of experience may be an illusion, like the world we experience in our dreams. To come to certain knowledge, we should proceed methodically, beginning with first principles, as in mathematics. To get to those first principles, we should question all that might be illusionary – Descartes' method of doubt. But, so he argued, when I doubt the veracity of my experiences, there is at least the "I" that does the doubting; "this proposition, *I am, I exist* is necessarily true whenever it is put forward by me or conceived in my mind." Hence, the French phrase *je pense, donc je suis*, an argument that has come to be known by the Latin phrase *cogito, ergo sum* – I think, hence the I that does the thinking, must exist. Once Descartes had thus established a foundation that could not be undermined by doubt, he also argued for the necessary existence of God, the reliability of mathematics, and thereafter also of the best results of empirical knowledge, stressing criteria such as clarity.[2]

Bacon and Descartes both acknowledged the possibility of error. Hence, they called for careful observation and rational analysis, features that, jointly, have become defining characteristics of modern science and humanities scholarship. Here we will consider *why* such knowledge would be desirable, also in the humanities. Thereafter, we will consider *what* it would entail for the scholar to aspire to value-free knowledge, or at least, knowledge that is reliable and trust-worthy – the role-specific responsibility of a scholar in the humanities.

Why would reliable knowledge of the natural and the social world be important at all? There is a practical need and a moral obligation. For millennia, people have been wrong about the nature of the moon, the planets, the stars and much else. So what? Such mistakes did not harm

1 Francis Bacon, *The New Organon* (Cambridge University Press, 2000), pp. 40–42.

2 René Descartes, *Meditations on First Philosophy, with Selections from the Objections and Replies* (Cambridge University Press, 2017), p. 21.

them. However, people have learned the hard way which plants and mushrooms are edible and which are poisonous. Knowledge of our more immediate environment has been a matter of life and death. Our immediate environment includes other humans, with whom we have to live. Some of those have power over us. It is especially in our dealings with other humans that we can be misled easily. Hence, the critical scholarly study of human affairs is as important as careful studies of food and medicine. If one is engaged in affairs in an unfamiliar environment, and misunderstands the words and behavior of one's host, business might be lost.

Seeking reliable knowledge is not only a matter of self-interest. Knowledge claims should be warranted, not only because otherwise they would not be useful. Otherwise, they would not deserve the honor of being regarded knowledge. Also, having sound knowledge is also morally important, as ideas may have consequences. In the nineteenth century the mathematician William K. Clifford wrote an essay titled "The Ethics of Belief." His first example was that of the owner of a ship who sends a ship with migrants out onto the sea, knowing that the ship is old and had needed repairs in the past. He overcomes his doubts, and comes to hold that the ship is seaworthy. When the ship goes down and the people perish, we judge that the owner has not just made a commercial mistake, which may be covered by an insurance policy. He has failed morally. Also, even if the ship had the luck that it crossed the ocean without an accident, the owner would have acted immorally by not securing adequate knowledge before allowing himself to believe that the ship was seaworthy. Clifford summarizes this in a stern normative principle: "it is wrong always, everywhere, and for anyone, to believe anything on insufficient evidence."

Being serious about knowledge claims applies not only in the technological sphere. Clifford considers a second example, about a group of believers deviating from established Christianity, as they neither believe in original sin nor in eternal punishment, doctrines taken serious in his Victorian era. The rumor was spread that they manipulated children and isolated these from parents and friends. The matter was investigated, and the accused were found to be innocent. The accusations had been based on insufficient evidence, and the accusers could have known this. The critics "*had no right to believe on such evidence as was before them.* Their sincere convictions, instead of being honestly earned by patient inquiring, were stolen by listening to the voice of prejudice and passion." Also, even if further inquiry would have shown that the adherents of this religious sect had misbehaved as accused, spreading the rumor would still have been morally wrong as long as the accusations were based on insufficient grounds.

Scholars of religions, cultures and literatures may feed the opinions of their audience about the people their studies focus upon. If their work is not based on good evidence but on prejudice and fear, their pronouncements are irresponsible. The search for good evidence should be the scholar's prime responsibility. Our beliefs regard others; collectively, our beliefs form the social web. "Into this, for good or ill, is woven every belief of every man who has speech of his fellows. An awful privilege, and an awful responsibility, that we should help to create the world in which posterity will live."[3]

A few decades after Clifford, the psychologist and philosopher William James argued for a more permissive attitude in an essay titled "The Will to Believe." He argues for the right to believe something that is not sufficiently certain, though he argues for that right only under certain conditions. A particular relevant case may be when embarking on a personal relationship. By believing someone to be well disposed toward you, even without having sufficient evidence yet, you may actually make that person treat you well. By explicating under what conditions, one's desires or preferences might be a decisive factor when forming one's beliefs, James implicitly acknowledges the priority of more objective knowledge whenever that is feasible.[4]

The stern idea that one should only believe that which has been established beyond doubt, is asking too much. We never have unquestionable knowledge, based on a solid foundation. Thinking of knowledge as a construction, Karl Popper developed in *The Logic of Scientific Discovery* the metaphor of foundations in a less absolutist way.[5]

3 William K. Clifford, 1879. "The Ethics of Belief," in L. Stephen and F. Pollock (eds.), *Lectures and Essays by the Late William Kingdon Clifford*, Volume II (London: Macmillan, 1879), 177–211, pp. 186, 179, 182.

4 William James, *The Will to Believe and Other Essays in Popular Philosophy* (New York: Longmans, Green & Co., 1897).

5 Karl Popper, *The Logic of Scientific Discovery* (London: Routledge, 1992), p. 94.

> Science does not rest upon solid bedrock. The bold structure of its theories rises, as it were, above a swamp. It is like a building erected on piles. The piles are driven down from above into the swamp, but not down to any natural or "given" base; and if we stop driving the piles deeper, it is not because we have reached firm ground. We simply stop when we are satisfied that the piles are firm enough to carry the structure, at least for the time being.

We can construct the building upwards and we can drive the piles deeper, but there is no absolute foundation. Nonetheless, as the city of Amsterdam shows, one can have a great city on soft foundations. In fundamental physics, theoretical physicists seek to develop theories about underlying realities, driving the piles deeper, while at the same time in the life sciences, colleagues are developing insights drawing on regular chemistry, as the current theories of physics are good enough for their work. We always rely upon assumptions and beliefs that for the time being are not questioned. At least we assume the meaning of the words in the language in which we report our work and assume the reliability of our equipment. When in doubt, we can take a second look, and reconsider our instruments or our terminology.

We ought to push as far as we can if the consequences of a wrong judgment are very serious. Returning to Clifford's example of the ship, Van Harvey emphasizes that the responsibilities of the ship owner are *role specific,* rather than universal as Clifford's maxim had it: Given that the owner earns the money from the people who board the ship, he is responsible for making sure the ship is safe.[6] The wide-ranging injunction of Clifford might be too demanding to live by fully, but his essay does convey a significant message about scholarly responsibility for ideas, as these may inspire actions and attitudes.

SCHOLARS: PERSONAL AND PROFESSIONAL VALUES

Engineers, lawyers, and doctors need malpractice insurance. The philosopher Daniel Dennett raised provocatively the question whether philosophers should have such an insurance too. He tells the story of

6 Van A. Harvey, "The Ethics of Belief Reconsidered." *Journal of Religion* 59 (1979), 406–420.

a virus introduced into a Third World country. The researchers thought they were doing something good, but the virus raised infant mortality, undermined health and well-being, and strengthened the power of the traditional despot who was ruling the country. The researchers defended themselves by arguing that their critics "were trying to impose 'Western' standards in a cultural environment that had no use for such standards."

These researchers were, in the narrative by Dennett, not coming from agricultural or biomedical sciences.[7]

> They were postmodern science critics and other multiculturalists who were arguing, in the course of their professional researches on the culture and traditional "science" of this country, that Western science was just one among many equally valid narratives, not to be "privileged" in its competition with native traditions which other researchers – biologists, chemists, doctors, and others – were eager to supplant. The virus they introduced was not a macromolecule but a meme (a replicating idea): the idea that science was a "colonial" imposition, not a worthy substitute for the practices and beliefs that had carried the Third-World country to its current condition.

The story illustrates a concern inspired by real events: The humanities have been abused to play down well-established knowledge. Thomas Kuhn's study *The Structure of Scientific Revolutions* has been claimed for such purposes quite often. Playing down well-established knowledge tends to serve those in power, according to Dennett, while being disadvantageous to women, to homosexuals, and to other minority groups.

Through the work of Thomas Kuhn and others, an all too optimistic view of science and scholarship has been exposed as illusory; knowledge develops through a social practice of fallible humans. Nonetheless, science and scholarship deserve to be seen as social enterprises that deliver genuine knowledge in a cumulative way.[8]

7 Daniel C. Dennett, "Postmodernism and Truth," in D. O. Dahlstrom (ed.), *Contemporary Philosophy: The Proceedings of the Twentieth World Congress of Philosophy, Volume 8* (Bowling Green, OH: Philosophy Documentation Center, 2000), 93–103, pp. 93 and 94.

8 Thomas Kuhn, *The Structure of Scientific Revolutions* (University of Chicago Press, 1962); Philip Kitcher, *The Advancement of Science: Science without Legend, Objectivity without Illusions* (Oxford University Press, 1993).

This regards not only the understanding of nature, but also of ourselves and our fellow humans, of history, culture, language, religion, and thought. Working with the best knowledge available and seeking to improve it further, is morally required. In this context, the natural and social sciences and the humanities are on the same side.

Studying humans should be done with academic integrity, an integrity that involves academic distance from commercial, political, and ideological interests. In *Merchants of Doubt*, historians Naomi Oreskes and Erik M. Conway have documented in detail how a few scientists have allowed themselves to be exploited by commercial interests from the tobacco and fossil fuel industry.[9] Dennett makes clear that such a violation of scientific integrity may involve philosophers of science as well, as they may have provided arguments used to undermine well-established knowledge. And so, too, for others in the humanities: Historical arguments have been used for nationalist causes; claims about religious traditions have served to persecute particular religious groups.

All research may have consequences beyond the scholarly domain. When art historians conclude on the basis of their research that a particular painting has been made by Rembrandt rather than by one of his students, this scholarly claim significantly increases the value of the painting. Such consequences are unavoidable, but financial interests should not have been a factor in their judgment. They should not say that it is by Rembrandt *in order to* raise its value. Nor, of course, should they deny artistic provenance, unless they have good scholarly reasons to believe that such is the case.

Whether one needs a malpractice insurance, depends primarily on the character of the society one is involved in. The more likely it is that people resort to litigation to protect their social or commercial interests, the sooner there is a need for malpractice insurances for scholars in history, religious studies, literary studies, art history, and other disciplines. Whether we need such a protective measure or not, scholars in the humanities should deliver the best possible knowledge,

9 Naomi Oreskes and Erik M. Conway, *Merchants of Doubt: How a Handful of Scientists Obscured the Truth on Issues from Tobacco Smoke to Global Warming* (New York: Bloomsbury Press, 2010).

given the way we humans in our subjectivity may err, are able to rationalize our preferences, and all too often fool others and ourselves. We need to establish the evidence and develop sound arguments as good as we can.

How high the bar is for "sufficient evidence," depends on the context and on the risk involved, that is, the potential consequences of policies based on those scientific and scholarly insights. As our conclusions always go beyond the data, the level of certainty required does involve the social context, opinions on the acceptability of the consequences of a potential mistake.[10]

But this is about the social consequences. The more general question is about scholarship itself. In brief: It seems that relevant scholarship should be "value-free," even though values, judgments, are involved throughout investigations. What, then, might one mean by aspiring to "value-free" scholarship, and why would such scholarship be valuable?

For the sake of this analysis, we will consider the role of value judgments in the humanities in a few ways. As with all other issues touched upon in this book, there is much more to be said about values than can be covered here.

As we study human practices and beliefs, we also study human judgments of many various kinds. Linguists may consider what in a particular context counts as correct use of language, and what does not. And this may itself have social consequences: having learned to use one's language in the right way, may promote social status, and hence create opportunities. In cultural studies, the study of "high culture" and of "popular culture" may involve various ideas about beauty, associated with different social standing.

Precisely because the practice studied – language use, cultural preferences – includes values, scholars studying such practices should be cautious so as not to copy the values of those studied. A scholar who studies the rhetoric and symbols of a racist movement, need not endorse the political opinions of those described and analyzed. So, too, when studying an emancipatory movement; the scholar should not let affinity undermine critical scrutiny. Even if a movement as a

10 Heather E. Douglas, *Science, Policy, and the Value-Free Ideal* (University of Pittsburgh Press, 2009).

whole is sympathetic to the scholar, a scholarly report is only credible if the scholar operates not as an advocate stressing the positive elements, but rather describes honestly the stronger moments and the weaker ones. In the professional role, a scholar should not be unduly influenced by personal antipathy or sympathy for those studied. Within the scholarly description and analysis, one should try to suspend *personal* judgments. In this sense, scholars in the humanities should aspire to do "value free" research, research that is not determined by the likes and dislikes of the scholar.

However, some reflections in the humanities are about our own judgments. Ethics, the philosophical reflection on normative judgments, is the prime example; so, too, for social and political philosophy and aesthetics. In philosophy, including ethics, scholarly analysis does not describe and analyze judgments made by others, as object of study, but argues what choices and judgments the philosopher considers worthy a defense or deserving of criticism. Neutrality in such a context cannot be neutrality about the outcome, as the aim is to come to a justified conclusion. Scholarly research would involve, however, the exclusion of personal preferences from the argumentative structure. Merely stating that I, as a scholar, prefer this over that, does not count as an argument. The value has to be argued for, and cannot be merely taken for granted.

Judgments, including moral judgments as well as more prudential considerations, may be unavoidable when it comes to the choice of topic for an individual scholar and the priorities that a funding agency or government sets. Some topics are deemed of interest as a deeper understanding of those issues might further scholarship. Some may be deemed such, but for now be laid aside as too difficult for the research to be fruitful. Other research questions may be promoted because they are considered relevant to society, or to particular groups within society. Whatever the motives for selecting a topic, the intent of those who set the topic is not to hear back from the researcher that this is an important topic to study; that would be reflecting merely the judgment made by selecting the topic. If scholars were paid to provide nothing but pronouncements desired by financial, political, or religious interests, it would be abuse of scholarship; think again of the example of *Merchants of Doubt: How a Handful of Scientists Obscured the Truth on Issues from Tobacco Smoke to Global Warming*. The aim should be to learn something about the topic studied, even when research is to the service of advice. If a government is seeking policy advice on an issue, it should be good scholarship that underlies the advice.

Thus, moral, aesthetic, and prudential judgments and personal preferences are involved in research, as they occur among those studied, as they may be held by scholars, and argued for or against by them, and as such judgments have determined the topics time is invested in. Precisely because the domain studied is laden with such judgments, a fair, unbiased scholarly assessment is of great value. That is how the paradoxical phrase "the value of value-free research" might be understood.[11]

Within scholarly research, operating according to *epistemic* values is not only unavoidable; it is positively desirable. An explanation has a strong claim to the honorific title of being knowledge when work is done carefully, exercising great care in the design and execution of the research, when the proposed explanation is specific and allows for precise predictions, fits well with what else we know (coherence) and avoids inconsistencies. Such considerations are epistemic, that is, knowledge-promoting.

Also, as scholarship is inherently *social*, there are attitudes and norms that promote collaboration and make it possible for others to check the conclusions.[12] Honesty and transparency about methods and data are key values, but so too is a safe working environment within which students and PhD candidates are encouraged to speak out, also against seniors on whom they may depend. Various organizations have developed Codes of Conduct for the integrity of research. The *Netherlands Code of Conduct* stresses principles such as honesty,

11 Robert N. Proctor, *Value-Free Science? Purity and Power in Modern Knowledge* (Cambridge, MA: Harvard University Press, 1991).

12 Ernan McMullin, "Values in Science," in P. Asquith and T. Nickles (eds.), *PSA: Proceedings of the Biennial Meeting of the Philosophy of Science Association, Vol. 1982, Volume Two: Symposia and Invited Papers* (University of Chicago Press, 1983), 3–24; reprinted in *Zygon: Journal of Religion and Science* 47 (2012), 686–709; Hugh Lacey, "Distinguishing between Cognitive and Social Values," in K. C. Elliott and D. Steel (eds.), *Current Controversies in Values and Science* (New York: Routledge, 2017), 15–30.

scrupulousness, transparency, independence, and responsibility; a European one reliability, honesty, respect, and accountability.[13]

That such social and epistemic values contribute to the reduction of error and help reduce bias in the evaluation of scholarly analysis gives "value free science" its value. By aspiring to exclude personal and political preferences while operating with social and scholarly integrity, science and scholarship help to weed out our biases and narrow mindedness, and hencc makes claims to knowledge worthwhile. Not that this is easy. Trust has to be earned, again and again.

How to do research in ways that reduce bias, an undesirable influence of one's own prejudices? I will limit myself to a few issues that have arisen in religious studies, my own primary window on the humanities. How might one be fair to those studied? How might one move beyond their self-understanding? Also, how, as a human with a particular perspective and personal convictions, might one remain "neutral" in one's scholarship? And to what extent does such neutrality imply respect for the views and feelings of those studied?

When studying religious groups, practices, and beliefs, a fundamental task is to understand the self-understanding of those studied. What do their actions mean to those involved? Why do they behave in the way they do? A fair description treats the people involved as actors, who lead their lives, who have intentions, ideas, and emotions. The aim is not empathy, providing an account of their experiences such that I come to share their feelings, but to understand their experiences and their own interpretations of their own experiences, in the context of their own ideas about the world they live in.

Thus, one might at first use *concepts of the actors* involved, concepts near to the experience, as understood by them in their own language and context. Thereafter, one might redescribe and understand the practices and beliefs in other terms, *analytical concepts*, further removed from the immediacy of the experience. If one were limited forever to experience-near concepts, one would not move on, and could not engage in comparative projects or other forms of analysis.

13 *Netherlands Code of Conduct for Research Integrity* (Amsterdam: KNAW, 2018). *The European Code of Conduct for Research Integrity. Revised Edition* (Berlin: ALLEA – All European Academies, 2017).

The approach described here is, in principle, bottom-up: from the particular cases the scholars moves on toward more general considerations about human cultures, as shaped by religious systems of symbols.

To some extent, what comes first is learning the way they use their own language, before embarking on translation or analysis. Once some knowledge of the language has been acquired, one might see patterns, perhaps noticing that some words function as verbs. The scholar could start to raise comparative questions about this language in comparison to others, or delve deeper into its pragmatics in spoken communication, perhaps by registering utterances in a phonetic script that is the invention of scholars, and totally alien to the script used by the speakers of that language. The scholar will have prior knowledge of the grammar of other languages, and thus be sensitive to particular phenomena, which thus are lifted up in the account of their self-understanding. Such a heuristic would work top-down. Nonetheless, the authority on the way they speak, think, and act is with those people themselves. In that conceptual sense, fair description comes first.

Though the basis is observation, describing their self-understanding already involves interpretation. As the anthropologist Clifford Geertz wrote in his essay "Thick Description: Toward an Interpretative Theory of Culture": "Right down at the factual base, the hard rock, insofar as there is any, of the whole enterprise, we are already explicating; and worse, explicating explications." By the way, Geertz came "into anthropology from a humanities background, and especially from one in literature and philosophy," as he let his readers know in his autobiographical *Available Light*. As I understand the humanities here, a culturally sensitive anthropology, such as his, can be included among the humanities (though institutionally it is often located among the social sciences), precisely because this discipline does take the perspective of the people involved seriously.[14]

Given the challenge by Geertz, my own emphasis on establishing the facts first is an overstatement. Facts are constructed by a process of

14 Clifford Geertz, "Thick Description: Toward an Interpretative Theory of Culture," in Geertz, *The Interpretation of Cultures: Selected Essays* (New York: Basic Books, 1973), 3–30, p. 9; Geertz, *Available Light: Anthropological Reflections on Philosophical Topics* (Princeton University Press, 2000), p. 11.

interpretation. Preliminary ideas, about the meaning of language, about humans being male or female, a child, or an adult, about the need for social structure, and much else are part of the scholar's input. As long as responsible scholars come to agree, we accept the facts as established. When doubt arises, we may need to have to push further, in a new round of reflection on our assumptions and the material available to us. That would correspond to "driving the piles deeper," to return to Popper's metaphor quoted above. But the main thrust would be to work with those facts, and build up our knowledge, through comparative studies and other forms of analysis.

There are some deep philosophical issues regarding knowledge and the categories we bring to the description. Despite this caveat, we still may hold that in common sense terms the facts deserve to come first. However, scholarship is more than merely recording the self-understanding of a particular group of people in their own terms. Scholars redescribe the beliefs and practices of those people with the help of the scholar's analytical tools and concepts, and thereby embed those beliefs and practices in a larger scholarly framework. There are many different approaches possible. Historical analysis, drawing on evidence of preceding stages, might be called for. Or one might study the way people shape their world by the words they speak, delineate groups and identities, claim authority or allegiance, as one might do in sociolinguistics.

Russell T. McCutcheon has made a strong demarcation between the role of the scholar of religion and the role of the believer or sympathizer. As he argues in *Critics Not Caretakers: Redescribing the Public Study of Religion*, believers, including theologians, provide data for religious studies, but they have no "monopoly on determining how their behaviors ought to be viewed (. . .). The participant's viewpoint, their behavior, and the institutions they build and reproduce are data for the scholar intent on theorizing as to *why* human beings expend such tremendous creativity and intellectual/social energy in discourses on the gods, origins, and endtimes." He focuses on discourses, on the language used, e.g. with a distinction between sacred and profane, and the social functions of such rhetorical distinctions. Other scholars may study religious practices in other ways. However, the general line for such scholarship is that studying religion should be distinguished from practicing religion. The scholar of religion should not become a spokesperson for particular insiders.

Scholarship on religion "helps us see something other than the timeless, unexplainable 'sacred symbols' and 'enduring values' that occupy the attention of many of our colleagues," at least, those that seek to appropriate such scholarship. Speaking of a book by Karen Armstrong, he writes: "In the end, then, and in spite of its impressive command of the data, *A History of God* is yet another instance of the liberal attempt to unify diversity by glossing over concrete difference of culture, politics, economics, and so on, in favor of a presumably abstract, nonhistorical – and, in this case – so-called religious or spiritual sameness." Thus, McCutcheon argues that the scholar should do more than merely describing what goes on or translating between insider self-description and public understanding; in theorizing, the scholar of religion offers a different perspective, and one that may not be welcome to those whose practices and beliefs are studied.[15]

A fable associated with his critical stance might be the one about the new clothes for the emperor, their non-existence exposed by a young child, not limited by obedient reverence. Is the scholar like the child, not hampered by reverence? But not every emperor parades while naked; the fable's conditions are the exception rather than the rule. The scholar need not be an obedient servant, a caretaker, but neither is it self-evident that the scholar always should assume the role of the critic who *evaluates* the life of others.

Calls for *respect* surround public debate and scholarship. One should not hurt the feelings of fellow humans. Of course, one should not hurt them for no reason at all. But the risk is that this becomes a defensive strategy that serves to keep unwelcome insight at bay. It was because some readers felt offended that Penguin felt they had to withdraw Wendy Doniger's book *The Hindus* from the market in India (see Chapter 3).

Charging that something is disrespectful, may be a way to keep unwelcome scholarship at bay. Seeking to avoid giving any offense, may undermine clarity, and more. Stefan Collini, a scholar in literary

15 Russell T. McCutcheon, *Critics Not Caretakers: Redescribing the Public Study of Religion* (Albany: State University of New York Press, 2001), pp. xi, xv, and 55.

studies, concluded his brief book *That's Offensive! Criticism, Identity, Respect* with the following encouragement not to engage in self-censorship to avoid giving offense:[16]

> When engaged in public argument on matters of ethical or cultural importance, do not be so afraid of giving offense that you allow bad arguments to pass as though they were good ones, and do not allow your proper concern for the vulnerable and disadvantaged to exempt their beliefs and actions from that kind of rational scrutiny to which you realize, in principle, your own beliefs and actions must be subjected. This is not an exhortation to be offensive, though it is an exhortation to be critical – an activity always likely to give offense. But, for others as for ourselves, there are many things worse in life than being offended, and being treated as incapable of engaging in reasoned argument and discrimination is certainly one of them.

Careful and critical studies of personal convictions may be challenging to those involved. However, just as in medicine, climate studies, or other areas of research important to our lives, we should welcome unwelcome messages, if those follow from serious research and are well supported by the available evidence. Those challenged by those insights should appreciate at least that being challenged shows that they are taken seriously.

The scholar has to respect the self-understanding of the people studied as their self-understanding, unless there is reason to suspect one is being fooled intentionally. However, that is the first stage, the gathering of data, as people who inform us of what their symbols, stories and words, their practices and beliefs mean to them, and how they understand a meaningful life. The scholar moves on, and uses those data in comparative and explanatory analysis. There are no limitations, *a priori*, for the perspectives the scholar might take. Except, it seems, for one: theology.

What is not available to the scholar of humanities, qua humanities scholar, is a theological stance. If the people appreciate a particular event as an appearance of Mary, the mother of Jesus, the humanities scholar takes that as a report about their beliefs, and might ask for the

16 Stefan Collini, *That's Offensive! Criticism, Identity, Respect* (London: Seagull, 2010), p. 66f.

resources that the believers draw upon in offering this interpretation. Or the focus might be on the psychological function those beliefs have for those in need. Or on the political authority that is challenged by appeal to a local divine revelation. In the humanities one may pay attention to the way a text, community, or person refers to the divine, or to anything else that transcends our natural and social world, but these remarks are treated as utterances by humans, as elements in the domain studied; references to gods, spirits, or demons, and assumptions about revelation as a way of acquiring knowledge, are not analytical categories and methods available to the humanities scholar as such. A scholar in the humanities need not deny the existence of God nor the personal significance of a novel. But taking a faith stance, one does not operate as a scholar in the humanities, but as a human being. What then should be the stance of the scholar? How to be fair and neutral, when engaging the convictions of people?

The role of a referee in sports can serve as a helpful analogy.[17] The person who acts as referee may have a preference for one team over the other team, perhaps enchanted by the way they play the game. Nonetheless, while serving as a referee, such personal loyalties and evaluations should be suspended. The referee should be neutral. However, the referee is not a passive observer either. The referee has an active role, but one limited to judgments appropriate to that role, given the rules of the game.

One has to avoid language that reflects prejudice. Deeming a belief superstitious or heretical, is a judgment made by some insiders against other insiders. The scholar, in the academic role, need not use such labels. As a scholar one has to suspend belief or disbelief. If someone expects to meet a lost lover again in heaven, the scholar need not dismiss the statement, but can explore how the statement functions for the speaker. As all such statements are statements made in this world, they may have observable consequences down here, whether one believes in heaven or not. The scholar, analogous to a referee, has to

17 Peter Donovan, "Neutrality in Religious Studies." *Religious Studies* 26 (1990), 103–115; reprinted in McCutcheon, *The Insider/Outsider Problem in the Study of Religion* (London: Cassell, 1999), 235–247.

be alert to personal prejudices that might distort professional neutrality, and actively seek to counter such bias.

Diversity within the scholarly community in terms of gender or ethnicity may help scholars to be more alert to potential bias. Transparency about one's data and analysis also allows others to challenge a scholar when there seems to be bias. Diversity and transparency thus support a role-specific neutrality in scholarship. As a human, the referee is also a citizen, a lover, and a member of various communities. In those capacities, the neutrality expected of the academic need not apply at all. But as a scholar, the professional role is not that of a religious figure, a priest or guru, an advocate for Christianity or for atheism. The rules are those of scholarship.

Scholarly neutrality is analogous to academic freedom, which is also best considered as role specific. It is freedom from pressures that should not influence one's scholarly research and teaching, as research and teaching are to be guided by norms that promote scholarship, as understood by the people in the discipline. It is not a freedom that extends beyond such professional bounds, as if an academic need not show up for work or may use resources of the university to advocate a particular political view. The freedom of a citizen, to advocate a cause considered worthy, should not be confused with academic freedom and academic responsibility, which is role specific. Academic freedom comes with accountability for the performance as a teacher and scholar.[18]

SIMILARITIES AND DIFFERENCES: INDUCTION, DEDUCTION, AND REDUCTION

For reliable knowledge, the role of the scholar is important, the effort to reduce bias by adhering to the relevant social and epistemic values, while suspending personal preferences. But also important is the kind of reasoning used in the humanities and in the sciences. In this respect, there are similarities and differences between the sciences and the humanities. Can the humanities discover underlying explications,

18 Stanley C. Fish, *Save the World on Your Own Time* (Oxford University Press, 2008); Fish, *Versions of Academic Freedom: From Professionalism to Revolution* (University of Chicago Press, 2014).

similar to those provided by the natural sciences? If so, how? What might be learned from philosophy of science, which has taken most of its examples from physics? We will consider here three issues: Knowledge by generalization (induction), knowledge that begins with an idea (hypothetical-deductive), and reductionism, when theories use terms that differ from those used to describe the phenomena.

Knowledge may be constructed by *induction*, generalization. All swans are white. Or rather, all the swans we have encountered so far, are white. From a European perspective, this was the case until 1697 when black swans were discovered to exist in Australia. Thus, "all swans are white" turned out to be false. That is a risk for generalizations; a single counter example undermines the conclusion. Nonetheless, for the humanities one can concur with what Clifford Geertz wrote about jurisprudence and anthropology: "they are alike absorbed in the artisan task of seeing broad principles in parochial facts." Despite the risk involved in induction, scholars derive general insights from multiple case studies.[19]

The idea that all swans are white, might be saved by arguing that the newly discovered bird is not really a swan, even though in all respects except for its color it resembles the swans we are familiar with. Such a defensive move would transform a claimed insight about the world ("all swans are white") into one that is true by definition, instructing us how we should use our words – if a bird is black, do not call it a swan. Such a move is often the response when scholarly insights uncovering diversity or history touches upon sensitive issues of identity; the status of the others is played down. "They" do not represent real Hinduism, or whatever is at stake. Such a dismissal imports a problematical normative assumption, about that which is to be taken as genuine, or who is to speak for the Hindus, the Christians, the Muslims, into the scholarly description of the human phenomena.

A second model of scientific reasoning, somewhat more sophisticated, is called *hypothetical-deductive*. One has an idea, a theory, a model, a hypothesis, as to how things might be. From this model, one may

19 Geertz, *Local Knowledge* (New York: Basic Books, 1983), p. 167.

derive predictions. If observations are at odds with the prediction, the hypothesis was wrong, and should be abandoned. If the observation matches the prediction, one may continue to entertain the hypothesis, at least for now. We can never be certain; our predictions may be at odds with future observations. Such vulnerability, also called falsifiability, is considered a strength rather than a weakness. Knowledge claims that are beyond potential dispute, think of conspiracy theories, are not really knowledge, but rather pseudo-science, according to the demarcation between science and pseudo-science proposed by Karl Popper.

However, falsification is not as straightforward as it may seem. Perhaps other assumptions were involved in the derivation of the prediction, and the failure could be due to one of those. Or the observation might be under conditions that are not precisely those assumed by the model. Perhaps, an additional assumption might give us an improved version of the theory. One might live with an anomaly, an exception, in the hope that future developments will resolve the issue. It is quite human, to try to save one's favorite theory, rather than to discard it at the first challenge, and some such patience is not against the scholarly ethos. Thus, Imre Lakatos came up with a view of scientific research in terms of research programs. Rather than discarding a theory that appears to have been falsified, researchers modify their theory. They may also have a particular idea about the way to develop their research program while protecting the core; such ideas he calls a *heuristic*, a search strategy.[20]

One might perhaps understand as a research program the idea that there has been, a period in history when in various cultural contexts a new orientation emerged, an Axial Age – an idea we will consider in greater detail in Chapter 6. At first, this may have appeared to be an inductive conclusion, on the basis of examples from China, India, Greece, and Israel. It may be challenged. What about Egypt or Japan? What about developments elsewhere, or in a different era? Are those developments sufficiently similar? Upon encountering such challenges, the idea that there has been an Axial Age is not abandoned, at least, not by all its adherents. It rather develops, as does the defense.

20 Imre Lakatos, *The Methodology of Scientific Research Programmes. Philosophical Papers, Volume I* (Cambridge University Press, 1978).

Exceptions are accommodated. Perhaps the claim is not about a global transformation, but about the emergence of something new alongside the "old," which continues to co-exist with the new. Perhaps the Axial Age is not a particular epoch, but rather a symbol for a type of cultural change. If its advocates operate thus, the idea may be maintained. The risk is that the idea might lose its relevance as it loses its original meaning; it might die by a thousand qualifications. A more positive understanding of this process, might be to understand the notion of an Axial Age as a heuristic tool, for some time helpful when we study complex historical developments in various places, but not itself a conclusion about the way things have been.

In the sciences, theories are often quite different, conceptually, from the phenomena described. For the air in a balloon or a bicycle tire, notions such as pressure and temperature may be understood in terms of moving atoms, bouncing against a wall. Such a model needs a bridge between the macroscopic description, in terms of pressure and temperature, and the microscopic one, in terms of a multitude of atoms, each with its mass and velocity. In this case, analyzing the pressure in a balloon in terms of bouncing atoms works very well; it is a successful *reduction* of a macroscopic description to a microscopic one.

Offering an explanation in terms that are different from those used to describe the phenomenon, is very common. As for the opposite: An explanation does not achieve much if it merely repeats the assertion to be explained, as when the sleep-inducing power of opium is explained by ascribing to opium a *virtus dormativa*, a dormitive principle – the example comes from *Le Malade Imaginaire*, a 1673 play by Molière. Though a modern explanation of the effects of opium is in terms of neurochemistry, opium still puts people to sleep; changing the terms does not undermine the reality of the phenomenon. Research may be reductionist, when one seeks to explain the sleep-inducing power in terms of known chemistry, or when a researcher seeks to develop a more advanced theory about underlying processes.

We may have to live with multiple descriptions, including the way we describe our own experiences alongside explanatory descriptions that are farther removed from ordinary experience. One way to articulate this for the natural sciences has been in terms of the distinction between a manifest image and a scientific image of the world.[21] The astronomer Arthur Eddington described in *The Nature of the Physical World* two tables in his study at home. The ordinary table is a solid brown one, made from wood. The scientific table is mostly emptiness; within that emptiness there are electrons rushing around at great speed. These two tables are one table, described in different ways. The two descriptions allow for the same behavior; I can place my dinner plate on it, and I can lean on it. The two descriptions are different but not incompatible. Though the scientific description does not eliminate the stability of the table, it does offer a rather different image of reality, at odds with common-sense ideas of substance.[22] So be it. If such a reductionist analysis of the table is adequate, we have learned how the table fits within our understanding of the world, and we have learned that a naive idea of substance is false. Such a reduction is a form of holism as it reveals the pervasive coherence of reality, in terms of chemistry and physics.

When a book is titled *Explaining Religion: Criticism and Theory from Bodin to Freud*, the reader may expect that the scholarly, explanatory redescription will deviate from religious self-description; so be it.[23] However, will it be an explanation such as the one in terms of neurochemistry for the effects of opium – introducing a rather different vocabulary and understanding of the mechanism involved? Or would it be an explanation such as the one of Santa Claus, undermining belief in this respectable figure from the North Pole? In the book referred to, the analysis draws upon psychology and sociology. It thus might explain that religious beliefs and practices serve communities and individuals in coping with life. It need not deny that religion does something for believers, nor should it suggest that they are dishonest about their beliefs. Thus, as with the sleep-inducing powers of opium explained by neurochemistry, the effects are real. However, such recognition might not be enough for the believer, who is attached to a particular description of the world, a description that includes one or more gods, who responds to prayers or offerings, who reveals insights,

21 Wilfrid Sellars, *Science, Perception and Reality* (London: Routledge & Kegan Paul, 1963).
22 Arthur Eddington, *The Nature of the Physical World* (New York: Macmillan, 1928).
23 J. Samuel Preus, *Explaining Religion: Criticism and Theory from Bodin to Freud* (New Haven, CT: Yale University Press, 1987).

who expects something of us. If such beliefs are important to a believer, a reductionist explanation that operates without reference to God or gods poses a challenge. Rather than being an innocent form of reduction, one that merely uses other terms than those of the believers, it becomes a competition between two sets of theories, as the descriptive account of the believer already included explanatory claims, such as that the gods are angry, or that God revealed what we should do, whereas the psychological, sociological, historical, and cultural explanations do without such a reference to gods. They need not deny the existence of God, but a scholarly understanding might challenge the self-understanding of the believers involved.

PATTERNS IN THE HUMANITIES: COMPARABLE TO LAWS OF NATURE?

There may be patterns in human history, culture, and languages. Some of those may be rooted in our biology or even in physics; the harmonious musical intervals that have characterized European music are well described by simple ratios of their frequencies, such as 2:1 – two tones that would be perceived as the same, merely differing by one octave. Some patterns may reflect similar needs in the social life of human communities. Also, some similarities in human practices may have arisen due to common origins of texts, languages, religions, and the like, or through trade and migration.

In 1446 a scribe copying a manuscript on Marco Polo's travels in Asia noticed that the story of the Buddha, mentioned by Marco Polo by a Mongolian name, was similar to the story about a Christian Saint from India, Josaphat. Legitimizing ascetic movements by stories about sons who leave their father's home, discover suffering in the world, and thereafter become world-renouncing ascetics, may have arisen independently more than once. In this case, however, scholars have uncovered a historical chain of transmission. Narratives about the Buddha were passed on via middle Persian into Arabic, and from there into Georgian, and subsequently into Greek and Latin. In the process, names changed and the religious frame was transformed into a Muslim one, and later into a Christian one, so that in the end the stories were about a Christian Saint, Josaphat. His name still resembles slightly the term *boddhisatva,* an incarnation of the Buddha seeking to serve humanity.[24]

Similarities are, by themselves, no definite argument for a common origin, as one should seek to trace the influence when such a dependence is suggested, but neither should we underestimate globalization long before the globalization of our time. But the other option is, of course, that there are genuine patterns to be discovered by the humanities, because there are general rules, "laws," about human nature and culture. How far does the similarity to the natural sciences go in this respect?

One major difference between laws of physics and patterns discovered in the humanities is in their character. Gravity is unavoidable. Humans have discovered how to fly, but not by transgressing the law of gravity. In designing airplanes, we have learned to work *with* the law of gravity. In contrast, one can decide to deviate from patterns discovered in the humanities. This is most typical in the arts. A composer might develop atonal music, that is, music that does not use the scale defined by the octave. By violating expectations, the composer creates something original.

Rather than laws of physics, one might perhaps think of patterns in the humanities as similar to political laws. The laws of a country can be violated, as these describe how one should behave, and not necessarily how all people do behave. Though there is this similarity, there is also an important difference between political laws and patterns uncovered in the humanities. Legal laws are prescriptive, how one ought to behave. Patterns in the humanities are sometimes perceived as prescriptive too; ordinary people often take grammar as determining how we *should* structure our sentences. But they are descriptive; they are discoveries about the way people use language. Language users have good pragmatic reasons not to stray too far from what is expected in a community; it makes it more likely that one is understood. But the poet who violates grammatical rules does not deserve a fine or prison sentence. The poem might be dismissed as gibberish, or it might be appreciated because of its original use of language.

24 Donald S. Lopez Jr. and Peggy McCracken, *In Search of the Christian Buddha: How an Asian Sage Became a Medieval Saint* (New York: Norton, 2014).

Patterns in the humanities are by themselves not binding, unlike physical laws. Nor are they prescriptive, as political laws. By becoming aware of them, we may decide to do something else. So too, by the way, in games. If your behavior is predictable, the opponent might notice. It thus might be to your advantage to deviate from a recognizable pattern. Not sticking to patterns might be a valuable strategy in some contexts. Playing around might be a human way to explore new options.

Anticipated patterns may become actual as we are aware of them, like self-fulfilling prophesies. If people expect that the bank will go bankrupt, they will withdraw their money, and indeed, the bank collapses; the prediction becomes true. But there are also self-denying prophecies, when justified expectations are undermined once people have become aware of them. The bridge is expected to collapse, people engage in repair, and the collapse is avoided. In the human sphere, insight about what might come to be, may be consequential. But the consequence need not be fatalism, as we can act intentionally, creatively against our predictions.

There is one more reason why patterns in the humanities, though respectable knowledge, do not have the same conceptual status as laws in the natural sciences. In the humanities, particular case studies continue to be important; these should have priority. However, one needs more than case studies. Otherwise, knowledge would be a mere aggregate of individual descriptions, like a toppled book case. Knowledge has some coherence, more than the mere alphabetical order of items in an encyclopedia. To display this coherence, it is selective rather than complete. A detailed description of all unique elements might be like a map of the country on a scale of one to one. Lewis Carroll, a mathematician known under this name as the author of *Alice in Wonderland*, wrote a brief dialogue on such a map in *Sylvie and Bruno Concluded*.[25]

> "We actually made a map of the country on the scale of *a mile to the mile*!"
>
> "Have you used it much?" I enquired.

25 Lewis Carroll, *The Complete Works of Lewis Carroll* (New York: Modern Library, 1939), 509–749, p. 617.

> "It has never been spread out, yet," said Mein Herr: "the farmers objected: they said it would cover the whole country, and shut out the sunlight! So now we use the country itself, as its own map, and I assure you it does nearly as well."

Detailed case studies may be overwhelming by their attention to detail. Also, they may be impractical when navigating the world. Presenting the world as structured according to patterns is useful to condense the richness of the world. Patterns may be heuristically necessary, as invitations to consider in another situation whether a similar pattern might be helpful in organizing the data. Finding patterns provides insights and opportunities for further research. But, in the end, the research has to regard the real world, and hence individual languages, texts, religions, and other human phenomena. So too for this book: while I aspire to describe "the humanities," all the areas of study included under this umbrella have their own characteristics, as reflections of their own disciplinary history and features of the phenomena studied.

In terms of the provisional definition of humanities as academic disciplines seeking *understanding of human self-understandings and self-expressions, and of the ways in which people thereby construct their world*, the quest for patterns is a development within that first "understanding." But as long as people understand themselves as actors, as beings who not only are objects of study but also can take such insight into account and thereby change their actions and self-understanding, the emphasis on patterns cannot be the final word in the humanities.

Humans figure twice in this definition, as object of study – the way they understand their own lives and their world – and as the scholars who seek to understand the practices and beliefs of those studied. However, those who are the objects of study may learn about the insights of scholars. They can respond; they are actors as well. Scholarly insights may be appropriated by some of those studied, and rejected by others, and thus come to serve in arguments between different strands within a tradition. Not only may the scholarly insights be challenging, but those about whom the scholars write, may challenge the scholars, questioning their scholarship, their methods and competence, the situated character of their scholarship. Even in historical studies about a distant past, there may be a response, not from those studied but from those who claim those historical events as "their own" history. Their insider perspective need not be the truth, though such responses to scholarship deserve to be taken seriously, as scholars can be biased too. Whatever the dislike or appreciation of insiders, the scholarly aim should be to come to knowledge that is as far as possible free of personal bias.

Part II

Who Needs the Humanities?

INSIGHTS FROM THE HUMANITIES AND ALUMNI OF ITS courses of study find their way into many professional domains. Education is basic to our society, teaching people to read and write, from the plain skills one learns in elementary school to more advanced skills in analysis and composition. Critical analysis of online sources, their rhetoric and their plausibility, is important for all citizens in our time. The humanities make people understand the world we live in, its history, languages, cultures, and places. Understanding others is of great importance in our world, in international relations, trade and tourism, but also at home, as we encounter persons who may have different experiences and convictions. Lack of cultural, historical, and linguistic competence and sensitivity may cost business. Not everyone needs to become a scholar in the humanities, but issues the humanities address are relevant everywhere, for us all, as citizens, as employees, and entrepreneurs, as humans.

How we relate to our past, how we understand ourselves, and how we relate to fellow humans: These are issues of great social importance. In Chapter 5, we will illustrate this with a reflection on law and religion, and the appeal to historical sources. The humanities are by humans, about humans, relevant to us, humans. Who are we? Chapter 6 will offer some reflections, on our existence as material beings, biological beings, cultural beings, technological beings, and planetary beings. Finally, Chapter 7 considers "the value of the humanities." Value as public value, in society. Also, as intrinsic value, a reflection on who we are.

5

Professionals

How to Live with Interpretations

How we relate to our past, how we understand ourselves, and how we relate to fellow humans: These are issues of great social importance. Such issues involve interpretation and appropriation. How should we understand texts from another era? This is not merely about understanding Homer's *Odyssey*; it also involves laws made a few years ago. Do they still have meaning and significance for us, who live in circumstances different from the time when those laws were formulated? Must we go back to the original meaning to determine their meaning for us, today? If not, what does give the law a meaning that is sufficiently stable to be relevant?

Similarly, in religion, an important facet of human identities: Should one go back to the origins of one's tradition and read the relevant scriptures as if they are immediately relevant for today, as fundamentalists of various stripes tend to do? If not, if we allow for ongoing interpretation and reinterpretation, as modernist believers are likely to do, can the tradition still provide a meaningful identity?

A scholar in the humanities may describe the meaning of a belief, practice, or text by going back to the original context and the intentions of the author. Is this also the appropriate approach for a professional, for a judge interpreting law, for a preacher invoking a biblical text, for a theologian speaking on the appropriate attitude toward artificial intelligence, for a literary critic articulating the meaning of a play by Shakespeare to reflect upon royal or pseudo-royal power today? Such professionals, and in many ways they stand for all of us, cannot avoid hermeneutical challenges. They engage in interpretation to cross the distance between that which has been handed down to us, our legacy – in art and literature, in architecture and civil arrangements, in law and as identities, whether religious or not – and our lives today.

How do insights from the humanities, about meaning and interpretation and about the dynamics of normative identities, relate to professional practices in law and in religion? That is the central question for this chapter. One particular dispute is whether the meaning of a text is the meaning it had in its original context, what the author intended, or whether we engage in continuing reinterpretation, a living tradition, and if so, how the results of such interpretative processes can be considered justified. This is an issue for scholars in literary and cultural studies, but even more is it an issue for legal and religious professionals who have to relate to documents from the past while addressing contemporary issues.

Religious texts from the past have a particular authority for members of a religious community; legal texts have a similar authority for the citizens of a particular state. Fundamentalists of various stripes claim that the first generations of Christians, the Prophet Muhammed and his companions, the Vedas, set the example that we should follow. A particular text is not just a text, but Holy Scripture, God's Word. Atheists often concur on such an originalist understanding of religion, concluding that therefore the text and tradition have to be dismissed altogether.

In legal contexts a similar issue may arise. A prominent example is the role the Constitution plays in the United States of America. How should it be understood, so that it still may have meaning for citizens today and thereby have authority over new societal arrangements? One particular point of view is *originalism*: the meaning of the Constitution, valid also today, should be the meaning it had at the time it was adopted. That seems to be in line with a prominent position in the discussion on scholarly interpretation in Chapter 2, the one by E. D. Hirsch, focusing on the author's intent.

How one should relate to the past, as significant for one's identity or as something we are glad to leave behind, is a normative question that involves methodological issues and more general philosophical concerns. In the end, this is not a scholarly question, given the freedom of political and religious communities and of individuals to decide on their own course. However, the way texts from the past are used is intertwined with discussions on interpretation, which can be illuminated by a humanities approach. In this chapter, we will consider these issues by focusing on a seminar where Dutch participants entered into a discussion with Antonin Scalia, at the time a judge on the United States Supreme Court, and with each other.[1] In *A Matter of Interpretation* Scalia had defended an originalist and textualist view of the meaning of legal texts. At the symposium, the Dutch philosopher Herman Philipse challenged Scalia, an outspoken Roman Catholic, by arguing that an originalist stance, applied not only to the Constitution but also to the Bible, would have to bring a reasonable person to opt for atheism.[2]

ORIGINALISM: BACK TO THE BIBLE AND THE CONSTITUTION?

In the Sermon on the Mount, as reported in the gospel according to Matthew, Jesus is told to have said with regard to the law:

> Think not that I have come to abolish the law and the prophets; I have come not to abolish them but to fulfil them. For truly, I say to you, till heaven and earth pass away, not an iota, not a dot, will pass from the law until all is accomplished. Whoever then relaxes one of the least of these commandments and teaches men so, shall be called least in the kingdom of heaven; but he who does them and teaches them shall be called great in the kingdom of heaven. For I tell you, unless your righteousness exceeds that of the scribes and Pharisees, you will never enter the kingdom of heaven.[3]

If there ever was a case of textualism in religion, we seem to have it here. Not even the tiniest letter, an iota, or even a dot, can be

1 Arie-Jan Kwak (ed.), *Holy Writ: Interpretation in Law and Religion* (Farnham, UK: Ashgate, 2009). This chapter is based on Willem B. Drees, "Not an Iota, Not a Dot Will Pass from the Law," 47–65 in this volume.

2 Antonin Scalia, *A Matter of Interpretation: Federal Courts and the Law* (Princeton University Press, 1997); Herman Philipse, "Antonin Scalia's Textualism in Philosophy, Theology and Judicial Interpretation of the Constitution," 15–45 in Kwak (ed.), *Holy Writ.*

3 Matthew 5: 17–20, Revised Standard Version.

disregarded when it comes to the Law, the Torah, the first five books of the Hebrew Bible.

Upon closer reading, the passage actually goes against textualism and originalism, as it is not the original text that is the norm, but rather righteousness, a broader and more flexible category, easily adaptable to new contexts. According to Matthew, this righteousness is to go beyond those who have become, with the unfairness characteristic of polemics among brethren, the archetypes of textualism and literalism, the scribes and Pharisees, that is, prominent non-Christian Jews in the first century CE. The opposition to textualism and literalism is even more explicit in the juxtapositions that follow the passage just quoted. Not only killing one's fellow is condemned, but even calling someone a fool makes one liable to the fires of hell. Not only adultery is criticized, but even looking at a woman lustfully. In these passages, the literalism rejected is literalism as a strategy that provides relaxation from moral challenges. In this context, the alternative to literalism is a stringent and demanding morality. This particular passage thus has inspired quite a few radical movements in Christianity, as well as liberals who exalted the Sermon on the Mount over ritual, legal, and magical texts elsewhere in the Bible.

In this chapter, we will consider interpretation in religion, and analogies or dis-analogies with legal and other forms of interpretation. I will argue that even though there may be good reasons for a modest preference for textualism in legal interpretation, arguments in favor of legal textualism do not carry over to support textualism in religious interpretation. If we look for an analogy for religious interpretation, we would do better if we were to look at political processes rather than at legal interpretation. Treating interpretation in religious traditions as analogous to legal interpretation may lead to fundamentalist misunderstandings, and all too easy atheist dismissal. Before coming to religious interpretation, I will first consider interpretation in legal contexts, in biblical scholarship, and in religious traditions.

Scalia argues against allowing judges too much freedom in re-interpreting laws. His concern is not only about democratic legitimacy and the separation of powers. A central question seems to be whether any other view of legal interpretation ascribes to words a stable meaning. Scalia writes dismissively on the alternative:

"The Living Constitution, a 'morphing' document that means, from age to age, what it ought to mean."[4] Thus, he emphasizes again and again *original* meaning.

Even if one does not agree fully with Scalia on textualism and originalism, his concern may be appreciated as reflecting a major feature of the rule of law. As alternatives to the rule of law one may think of *chaos*, when government collapses, and of *autocratic personal* leadership "above the law," when someone's personal preferences, interests and moods determine decisions. In contrast to chaos or autocracy, an advantage of the rule of law is its predictability, which allows one to anticipate consequences of actions one might consider. Another advantage is its validity for all within the range of this rule of law, unless grounds for discrimination are given in the laws, for instance when persons under a certain age are not allowed to drive cars. Predictability and generality make the rule of law greatly preferable over unrestrained flexibility in judicial interpretation.

Therefore, so Scalia's position, the rule of law requires originalism. Let me briefly define the way I will use this term and two terms associated with it, textualism and literalism.

> *Originalism* refers to the conviction that words and sentences are to be understood as they were understood originally, that is, at the time when the law was agreed upon. (A colleague in literary studies pointed out to me that in her scholarly community, the term "originalism" could have the opposite meaning, referring to a novel interpretation, one that is original. Here, however, "originalism" is used for the focus on the initial context.)
>
> *Textualism* is used as a label for the conviction that one should appeal only to the text of the law, rather than to other sources such as legislative history.
>
> *Literalism* means that one assumes the literal meaning of words to be the relevant one, rather than understanding the words as metaphors or indirect allusions.

Literalism may be appropriate in law, as the genre of legal texts is clearly not, for instance, that of poetry that plays with ambiguity of meaning, or irony that uses words while evoking a contrasting

4 Scalia, *A Matter of Interpretation*, p. 47.

meaning. With respect to legal interpretation, the main question I have is whether the choice has to be limited to one between originalism and *unrestrained* flexibility. There may be additional considerations such as consistency with earlier decisions and with other laws, while new factual considerations due to new technologies may have a major impact. Some flexibility seems needed in any case.

How can one allow for new interpretations while at the same time providing continuity and predictability? One strategy might be to explicate general principles that provide the background to specific rules. If one can argue that certain principles might have been behind the law at hand, such principles may guide the application of the law in circumstances not foreseen at the time the law was decided upon. Thus, a law that deals with privacy regarding letters in traditional mail might involve general ideas about respect for privacy, and those more general ideas may be applicable to email and to text messages on the smartphone as well. Such a trajectory of interpretation, though not always easy to execute, would not amount to "anything goes," and thus would not suffer from the extreme forms of indeterminacy of meaning that Scalia ascribes to the idea of a Living Constitution.

Even if one were to accept textualism and originalism with respect to legal interpretation, the law itself is not beyond change. Changing the terms of a social contract is a different matter from living according to the social and legal contract as it is at any given time. Such change is a matter of politics, rather than of legal interpretation. Thus, Scalia considers it proper that the Nineteenth Amendment to the United States Constitution, which gave women the right to vote, was adopted by the States. Giving women the right to vote was the result of a political process, as it should be, rather than the result of a decision by judges who by a creative interpretation would have argued that the original Constitution had intended to give women the right to vote, as if the Constitution had been misunderstood for well over a century.

Let us turn to religion. How is the dilemma of definite meaning, anchored in the past, and flexibility for the sake of later relevance to be handled there? Must a believer be an originalist with respect to the meaning of the texts? One of the colleagues in the seminar with Scalia argued that an originalist understanding was necessary, and that, when combined with honesty and acceptance of science, unavoidably it would lead to atheism. The philosopher Herman Philipse, himself an advocate of atheism, argues that a believer *qua believer* (rather than as a historian) has to be originalist. He calls this the Argument from Divine Authority.[5]

> Surely, the Christian believer may say, if the Bible really contains God's word, readers do not have any *authority* to interpret this Word otherwise than by using the methodology of Textualism or Originalism. The reason is that God's authority is absolute and that, God being eternal, omniscient and perfectly good, he will have formulated his final revelation in the New Testament precisely as he meant it, so that it is valid for eternity.

In the Argument from Divine Authority there is a major ambiguity. For a believer, there is no need at all to conflate the Author with the author, that is, to assume that the text which came to us via human authors has been intended literally by the divine Author. Many biblical books clearly present themselves as testimony by human witnesses rather than as perfect records. Also, a loving parent may well speak to his children in a way that is suitable to the abilities of the children, and so, too, for God's communications with the people. Furthermore, a God who truly loves a free human response may present us with interestingly ambiguous words. Or God intended the text to have multiple meanings to be uncovered by allegorical interpretation, with a moral and mystical meaning alongside the literal one. Or, to quote a remark by Aurelius Augustine, a major theologian of early Christianity, in his *De genesi ad litteram* (On the literal meaning of Genesis), we may have to do with "words that have been written obscurely for the purpose of stimulating our thought."[6] Thus, it might be that the Authorial intent is not expressed straightforwardly in the text.

A modern-day originalist (and an atheist philosopher who imposes originalism on others) who takes care to study with scholars in the humanities the formative period of Christianity will come to note that believers and theologians in early Christianity were neither originalist nor textualist. Different versions of the gospels existed side by side.

5 Philipse, "Antonin Scalia's Textualism," p. 35.

6 Aurelius Augustine, *The Literal Meaning of Genesis* (New York: Newman Press, 1981), Bk. 1, 20, 40.

Available material was revised in light of later needs and convictions. The early tradition displays substantial flexibility. This results in an interesting logical puzzle for someone who assumes that the initial believers and their later brethren should have been originalists: The originalist position is self-referentially incoherent. Such a critical challenge builds upon knowledge of the early tradition, upon humanities scholarship. In the next section, we will consider in more detail what the humanities may have to say on the interpretation of religious texts, beliefs, and practices. We will begin with biblical studies, and thereafter turn to other considerations regarding the role of texts in religions. Thereafter, we will move to the question relevant professionals have to face, how we in our time might use texts from a different time and place.

HUMANITIES SCHOLARS MUDDY THE WATERS

Many specialists in biblical studies understand their work as *historical* scholarship. They are not theologians but historians, trying to uncover the meaning of the text in its original setting, from the perspective of the original human author and for the audience it was addressed to originally. Whether they sympathize with the attitudes and visions expressed in the texts studied, is not an issue within their professional work. In the terms used here: Professionally they are originalists, though they are neither textualists nor literalists.

They are *originalist* as they seek to understand words and sentences as these were understood then. There are many complications as to what would be the original setting, especially if texts have formed over a long period, but here we will bypass such complications. The historians are text-oriented, but they should not be *textualist* in the sense given to the term above. If archaeological excavations or Hellenistic sources were to uncover facts relevant to the interpretation of passages of the Sermon on the Mount, they will include such insights into their interpretations of the original meaning of this text. It would be totally against the professional ethic to disregard *text-external* evidence on the basis of a textualist preference. For the honest historian, one needs something like *textualism plus*, taking into account texts and all other available evidence regarding the original context.

Historians are *not literalists* either. A historian may well have good reasons to understand a particular passage in a text as a rhetorical overstatement, as poetic license, as a song of praise, or whatever. If one is to understand a passage as it was meant in its initial context, one has to grasp the *genre* as intended in the original setting. The passage from the Sermon on the Mount with which we began this chapter may well be an evocative rhetorical composition, where overstatement is a figure of speech, used intentionally. If so, this passage in the Gospel according to Matthew would be misunderstood if regarded as if it were a balanced treatise on the proper interpretation of the laws of ancient Israel. Even the word "law" is to be understood carefully, as its genre is not law in our sense. It refers to the Torah, the first five books of the Hebrew bible, a diverse set of narratives and instructions, mentioned here in one phrase together with the prophets, the subsequent books on gifted leaders and critics of the people of Israel. Thus, an originalist sensibility to the word "law" undermines a modern literalist reading. The meaning in the original context is not always the literal meaning of the word.

In institutes of religious studies, we not only have historians of the texts, who may have an originalist interest, such as the archetypical biblical scholar depicted above. We also have historians of religions, who study religions as lived in the past and present. Sociologists, anthropologists, historians of religion, and others also engage in religious studies; religion being for them the object of study, not a methodological norm. They have revealed a bewildering variety of religious behavior. We should not be misled by the forms of organized religion most familiar to us, and this also regards the focus on the meaning of texts. In certain traditions rituals are far more important than texts. A theory in the history of religions suggests that ritual chronologically came first, with mythical narratives and creeds as subsequent stages of rationalization, while systematic articulation as dogma would be an even later development. Also, "words" used in meditation, *mantras*, are not necessarily words with a definite meaning.[7] They are recited; their performative function, and perhaps even their physical effect on the way we breath, is dominant. For a Muslim

7 Robert Segal (ed.), *Myth-Ritual Theory: An Anthology* (Malden, MA: Blackwell, 1998); Frits Staal, *Words without Meaning: Ritual, Mantras, and the Human Sciences* (New York: Peter Lang, 1990).

who does not understand Arabic, the Qur'an is, nonetheless, the holy book, to be recited in Arabic. Around the world, people do many different things with texts. Texts are written on slips of paper that are pounded and digested. They are written on banners that move in the wind. The holy book is displayed, elevated, and adored as an object of devotion. Jews may dance with Torah scrolls. Texts are used in ways only remotely related to reading.

In the Western world creeds have become a prominent characteristic of churches. In Protestant churches a propositional understanding of the canon, the Bible, is dominant. However, historians of religions discover again and again that for canonical texts, reading the actual text, in our modern sense of reading, is the exception rather than the rule. A text-oriented bias has been furthered by philosophers, linguists, and others in the academic study of religion, as exemplified by the interest in *The Sacred Books of the East*, as academics too tend to focus on texts, and besides, many came from Protestant parts of Europe. Working with texts suits the habits and preferences of academics. But it is one-sided; texts can be major sources of information, but concentration on texts is an unwarranted reduction of the object of study, living human religions.

Though texts and their semantic meaning are not as prominent in living traditions as it may seem at first, it is pertinent here to address the way texts are and have been interpreted within those religious strands that do give a major place to particular texts. There is an enormous diversity in ways in which texts from earlier periods were made relevant at a later time or in a different situation.

Allegorical interpretation, moving beyond the literal meaning of terms by understanding the text as coded language, has been widespread. Shifting the genre, and thus reading a text as poetry though it may have been a detailed instruction regarding sacrifices, is another option. Selective reading, distinguishing between a core and more peripheral texts, is a third option, selecting, for instance, the Sermon on the Mount as the one that should guide interpretations of other passages. Rereading the whole through a particular lens, such as rereading the Hebrew Bible as anticipating Christ is a fourth option. Adding an authoritative structure that guides the process of interpretation, such as an oral tradition (Hadith alongside the Qur'an, oral

Torah, etc.) or an authoritative papacy is another common pattern. And so on, and so forth. Historians of religions reveal a huge variety of processes of interpretation.

Most such processes of interpretation of ancient texts are at odds with modern academic sensibilities. They are also offensive to some participants within the traditions concerned. Within religious traditions there always have been voices against too much flexibility in interpretation, for instance against allegorical interpretation and against the role of ecclesiastical authorities mediating the interpretative process, as in the Protestant Reformation's call *ad fontes*, back to the sources, bypassing later interpretations. However, such critics also had their own ways of shaping the interpretative process according to their theological presuppositions.

Fundamentalism is a label used for a variety of movements that desire purity in interpretation, as literalist, originalist, and textualist as possible. Can and do they realize their ambition? Not, if we consider the pamphlets *The Fundamentals*, after which fundamentalism took its name. These were published in the early twentieth century, and sought to articulate the fundamentals of Christian belief. Within this project there have been interesting nuances with respect to the way the Genesis story of origins was interpreted. George Frederick Wright, who wrote the pamphlet that dealt with origins, was a Christian minister but also a prominent amateur geologist who had discovered and described deposits of the Ice Ages in the United States. Wright argued, in line with other conservative theologians, that the biblical authors did not know more about science, history or philosophy than others in their time. The Bible is inspired in what we need to know, believe, and obey for the sake of our salvation. The creation story of Genesis deals with the fact *that* God created, and not with *how* God created. In his contribution for *The Fundamentals*, in 1910, he wrote that all humans descend from a single, divinely created couple. However, in a publication two years later he wrote that humans are genetically related to the mammals. Evolution was for him not opposed to "special creation"; God could have been guiding the evolutionary process.[8]

8 Ronald L. Numbers, *The Creationists: From Scientific Creationism to Intelligent Design* (Cambridge, MA: Harvard University Press, 2006), pp. 33–50.

Fundamentalism in the first half of the twentieth century actually was opposed to literalism. William Jennings Bryan, leading spokesperson of the anti-evolutionist movement in the USA in the 1920s, wrote in 1923: "The only persons who talk about a twenty-four hour day in this connection do so for the purpose of objecting to it, they build up a straw man to make the attack easier, as they do when they attack orthodox Christians of denying the roundness of the earth, and the law of gravitation."[9]

Fundamentalism has many faces. Many adherents have a Western-style education in applied sciences: "many fundamentalists, especially in what might be called the middle management leadership of the movements, have obtained degrees in engineering, in medical technology, or in other technical scientific disciplines. By contrast, one finds few fundamentalists trained in astrophysics or other branches of science that are less empirical and more speculative and theoretical in orientation."[10] And even less, I surmise, with a genuine humanities training. Engineers promote a literal understanding of the texts without much concern for the historically situated character of those texts and the rich tradition of interpretations. They read religious texts like manuals rather than as texts that may be in various genres. In doing so, they depend upon relatively modern ideas about knowledge, rather than on an allegedly pure, original understanding of their own tradition. Fundamentalism is not the continuation of an old tradition, but rather a recent invention that breaks with the flexibility typical of religious interpretative processes. Fundamentalism is not originalism, but a particular form of modernism.

Philipse appeals for his link between religious belief and textualism to Augustine, whom he quotes indirectly: "Nothing is to be accepted save on the authority of the Scripture, since that authority is greater than all the powers of the human mind."[11] However, the passage quoted actually does not say in which way Scripture is to be interpreted. Appealing

9 Numbers, *The Creationists*, p. 58.

10 Gabriel Almond, R. Scott Appleby, and Emmanuel Sivan, *Strong Religion: The Rise of Fundamentalisms around the World* (University of Chicago Press, 2003), p. 124.

11 Philipse, "Antonin Scalia's Textualism," p. 35.

to Augustine for a textualist and originalist view grossly distorts Augustine's view on exegesis.

Augustine is open to *allegorical* interpretation. Even in *De Genesi ad litteram*, which by the title mistakenly might be taken to opt for a literal reading, Augustine uses allegorical interpretation in which historical realities are interwoven with transhistorical ones. Thus, references to Jerusalem relate the actual city to the heavenly realm. Sarah and Hagar, two wives of Abraham who really existed, according to Augustine, also stand for the Old and the New Testament. The lamb that is slain with Passover refers to a genuine sacrifice and meal, a lamb that is eaten, but also stands for Jesus Christ.[12]

Augustine's literalism is not literalism. The meaning for him is not the meaning in the historical setting when the text was formulated, as the claim that Augustine held to originalism suggests, but rather the meaning of the text as an allegorical description of history. Augustine did not use the word "literalism" in a way that we would recognize as literalist. Actually, here we are far removed from any literalism, as even a cursory reading of Augustine's commentary reveals. The meaning intended by the author is not to be taken in literalist fashion, given the religious and metaphysical views held by Augustine. He actually opposes literalism. For instance, when the text writes that God brought all the beasts and birds to Adam to see what he would call them, "we should not imagine God bringing the animals to Adam in a crudely material way," given the distinction between creatures and Creator.[13]

Furthermore, Augustine carefully handles the possibility of knowledge at odds with religious interpretations. He allows that he may be mistaken, as there is a genuine human component to our understanding of Scripture. For various passages he offers multiple possible interpretations. When Augustine comes to discuss the light on the first day, according to the narrative in Genesis 1, preceding the creation of the Sun as the source of ordinary light, he writes that we can take it literally as "the existence of material light, celestial or supercelestial, even existing before the heavens." But if we were to discover that this did not happen in such a way, we should acknowledge that "this teaching was never in Holy Scripture but was an opinion proposed

12 Augustine, *The Literal Meaning of Genesis*, Bk. 8, 4, 8.
13 Augustine, *The Literal Meaning of Genesis*, Bk. 9, 14, 24.

by man in his ignorance."[14] In case of an apparent conflict with well-established knowledge, Augustine warns the believer not to stick to a problematic exegesis, whether literalist or not, but rather encourages his readers to acknowledge that so far the text has not been understood correctly. Whatever the distance between the text and the divine Author, there certainly is a distance between the text and all human exegetical attempts, a distance that undermines any straightforward textualism, originalism, and literalism.

Let me formulate a conclusion on textualist and originalist options in theology. The fundamentalist idea that the early tradition was textualist, originalist and literalist is at odds with modern scholarship on the history of Christianity and the history of religions in general. Thus, if one makes the early tradition normative, one should not be a textualist, nor a literalist, nor an originalist.

A similar argument against originalism can be raised for originalism in relation to legal interpretation. Originalism appeals to the historical context in which a particular law came into existence. But understandings of the historical situation can be disputed, and often are. Just to consider one American example, a case against the District of Colombia, that is, the capital Washington, DC, which had prohibited the possession of handguns. The Second Amendment to the Constitution reads: "A well regulated Militia, being necessary to the security of a free State, the right of the people to keep and bear Arms, shall not be infringed." Justice Scalia argued that historically, at the time of the adoption of this Amendment, the right to self-defense was seen as an individual right, and hence the clause about the militia was not limiting the right to possess arms. Another Justice, John Paul Stevens, made an extensive historical argument as well, lifting up the initial phrase on a well-regulated militia, understanding the amendment being "a response to concerns raised during the ratification of the Constitution that the power of Congress to disarm the state militias and create a national standing army posed an intolerable threat to the sovereignty of the several states."[15]

14 Augustine, *The Literal Meaning of Genesis*, Bk. 1, 19, 38.

15 See Donald Drakeman, *Why We Need the Humanities: Life Science, Law and the Public Good* (Houndmills, Basingstoke: Palgrave Macmillan, 2016), pp. 79–81, quoting Justice Stevens from *District of Columbia* v. *Heller*, 554 US 570 (2008).

In the end, it was not knowledge of the historical context, but a five to four majority of the court that in 2008 decided on the interpretation of the Second Amendment. Historical references may play a role to articulate one's position, but that is history as selected, interpreted, and appropriated, if not even "reenacted." The term "re-enactment" is used for current use of history by historian Jill Lepore in her book *The Whites of their Eyes: The Tea Party's Revolution and the Battle over American History*. Her book emphasizes those who draw on history, as they interpret it, thus read into history their political views. To Lepore, "originalism" in constitutional interpretation is comparable to astrology.[16] As in the religion case, the problem is that one reads into history a message or pattern that is ours rather than theirs, more interpretation than a clear and relevant fact.

One need not be a believer, but unlike Philipse I hold that an honest believer can be a non-textualist and still with fairness can claim to be standing in a particular tradition. To avoid limiting myself to Christian examples: the authors of *Modern Muslim Intellectuals and the Qur'an* are Muslims who find within their own tradition resources for a contextual, historical understanding of their own tradition and a relevant modern interpretation of the Qur'an.[17] Denying them membership of their tradition, means that the argument in favor of textualism rests upon a particular choice of who is granted membership in a religious community, a choice on orthodoxy and heresy, a choice that is not one scholars should make.

UNAVOIDABLE CIVIC RESPONSIBILITY: LIVING RELIGION AND LIVING LAW

The normative texts of various traditions have problems with *internal* and *external consistency*. A snake that speaks, six days of creation, Jesus walking on water: What to do with such elements? Their strangeness is not always due to new insights; I am convinced that walking on

16 Jill Lepore, *The Whites of Their Eyes: The Tea Party's Revolution and the Battle over American History* (Princeton University Press, 2010), p. 7 (re-enactment) and p. 124 (astrology); that originalism resembles astrology is discussed by Drakeman, *Why We Need the Humanities*, p. 12f.

17 Suha Taji-Farouki (ed.), *Modern Muslim Intellectuals and the Qur'an* (Oxford University Press, 2004).

water was never perceived as ordinary. The story may have been told in this way precisely because the described phenomena were contrary to experience, and thereby would express the significance the figure of Jesus had for those who told the story. *Completeness* is even less to be expected. Would the Bible offer direct guidance on questions that emerged much later, say on genetic modification? Is it to be expected that the Qur'an answers clearly the question whether Muslims can participate in the political process in pluralist European societies? Believers at later times cannot avoid tension between the *authority* ascribed to the text and its *relevance for believers* at later times.

A scholar in the humanities need not be troubled by this challenge. As a historian, one might wonder what the text meant to people at an earlier time, while granting that this is not consistent with modern knowledge and values, nor helpful in addressing new moral challenges. As a historian of religion, one might describe the multitude of interpretational moves used in various epochs, to preserve or create relevance, for readers at those times. Such a historian of religions is interested in meanings *others* have attached to texts, irrespective whether they did so on good grounds or not. As indicated above, the scholar might find through research that most believers have not been originalist with regard to texts they inherited and used to understand and guide their lives; they gave the resources of the tradition a meaning relevant to them. The scholar of religion need not advocate or condemn this; it is an observation on what believers have been doing.

The challenge between the dated character of the text and its assumed relevance for believers today is a challenge for believers, and in particular for theologians – professionals who seek to speak to the people *in our time*, while referring to texts from a different era. What might it mean for contemporary believers "to keep the Sabbath," or the Sunday, as a day of rest? What about injunctions to care for widows and the poor? And on issues not mentioned in ancient texts: How should we respond to climate change? To be guiding believers today, the text needs to have a meaning. To be relevant for today, the meaning cannot be merely the meaning the text had long ago. Tensions between normativity and relevance drives the multitude of interpretational tricks considered above. How to respect the text, while also have it speak to us, in a different context, with questions not addressed in the text?

Though there are also non-cognitive ways that people live with stories, songs, fables, parables, and other texts, for some the question is how to understand those texts in our context, as texts that are still meaningful and authoritative for their community of believers. That seems to be the situation where the parallel with legal interpretation is most relevant. This brings us to normative, systematic considerations about the options we consider rightfully available to believers when such believers in a living tradition combine the normativity of the heritage with flexibility in order to remain relevant in changing circumstances.

A living tradition has to combine its heritage of texts, practices, and oral traditions, with freedom for further development, or at least application. If there is no concern for the heritage, it would not be a tradition but an invention *ex nihilo*. Here I will offer a model that describes how a theologian might appropriate texts from long ago for us today, thus moving beyond the task of the humanities scholar, who would be inclined to speak of their meaning for others, the original audience, or later recipients in ongoing reception history.

A scholarly responsible theologian would have to be open to a historical understanding of the heritage. That heritage consists in part in texts. Concern for the meaning of these texts gives originalism a place in religion, and, in this respect, the semantic meaning is its scholarly meaning, the meaning a historian would uncover. This originalism need not imply literalism, as said above, as a proper historical reception of the text also requires recognition of its genre. Thus, one understands the text primarily as a theological and religious expression in a particular historical context. For instance, the gospels are understood as written during the Roman era, some decades after the death of the Palestinian Jew Jesus, for communities of people inspired by him, and not as speaking immediately to us. Nor are they eyewitness accounts of that which the text purports to be about, the life of Jesus. Rather, they are human responses and theological articulations, telling the story of Jesus as interpreted and appropriated by individuals and communities through the lens of their situation and interests and the intervening developments. Thus, there is already a genuine distance between the text and the events the text is about. If we allow for the historically dated and context-related character of the text and seek to advocate particular beliefs, we may be interested in what moved those humans who finalized the texts.

So far, I described the understanding of the past, of the texts and the underling concerns and experiences. The theological task is application, or rather, appropriation, the articulation of possible meaning and relevance for the community of believers today. A contextual understanding of the original meaning might help; a text is understood as one that was meaningful to humans who faced particular challenges, or who wanted to articulate their anger or gratitude, and so on. In as far as we recognize some of their emotions and motives or come to agree with some of their moral concerns, their writings may become significant to us. When we formulate our own worldview, we may be formed and informed by the texts and our understanding of the original motives. But we should also acknowledge that we have come to see issues differently, whether factually or morally, say on slavery or the position of women. As I see it, a responsible theologian cannot avoid being selective and creative, and thus needs to be honest about the choices made. We, later readers, cannot evade responsibility for what we appropriate and what we pass by, or even reject.

That is, the texts, rituals, songs, and other elements of the tradition may shape the identities of later believers, up to the present, but just as with a family legacy, each generation and each individual again has to make the tradition his or her own, and in doing so, makes choices as to how it is appropriated. When a believer is challenged to justify why a particular commandment is applicable in a particular setting, and why certain other elements of the heritage are not applicable, one cannot just refer to the original text, as it is not the original text that does the selection or interpretation, but it is the reader who makes use of those texts and lets himself or herself be inspired by them. Even a fundamentalist who claims to be following the original and literal meaning of the text, is, in fact, interpreting and selecting. If one considers the Bible authoritative for one's life and actions, it may seem as if responsibility for my actions has been located in the Bible, but one should not miss the intervening link: The believers who have ascribed to the Bible, as they interpret it, such authority over their life and actions. Thus, in the end, the believer has full responsibility for this decision.

In such an understanding of religious interpretation as appropriation, all the relevant criteria of originalism and "textualism plus" with respect to an historically informed understanding of the text are respected, as one acknowledges the meanings of the text in relation to the historical context in which it arose. There is no naive reading into the text of new meanings. That is the scholarly part. But the second step is the existential part, the question whether one recognizes some of the experiences and messages conveyed by the text as relevant and existentially meaningful for us, as relevant for today. The text is not automatically normative, but at most *formative*; it becomes normative only in as far as it is appropriated as such.

Thus, flexibility at the level of the texts and discontinuity in worldviews may well be combined with recognition of some of the experiences of predecessors, without thereby being limited to their worldview. Religion is not just about the author's intentions, which need not be the Author's intentions. Religion is not primarily an interpretation of something given in the past. Rather, the faith of a believer may be articulated in conversation with the past. In making statements about the past issues of historical interpretation arise, but most religious utterances, even if they appear to be interpretations of the past, should be construed as current utterances.

At the symposium on interpretation in law and religion, Antonin Scalia and Herman Philipse both argued for an originalist reading of religious and legal texts. They both opposed a more dynamic view of interpretation, here argued for. My position is similar in structure to the defense of "living law," which Hans Nieuwenhuis, law professor and former judge on the Supreme Court of the Netherlands, offered at the symposium. He described law as a continuous speech act. By repeating words of predecessors, the present-day legislature reaffirms the law, and by reaffirming it now, they do so in a way that integrates current meanings into the meaning of the law.[18]

In understanding religion and law in such a way, one may rightly question whether it deals with interpretations that are *academically*, *historically* correct, the domain for which originalism seems to be the honest option. In my understanding, they should not be incorrect, if proper consideration is given to issues such as genre and context.

18 Hans Nieuwenhuis, "How to Handle a Living Constitution?" 131–145 in Kwak (ed.), *Holy Writ*.

However, religious and legal practice should not to be understood as historical studies in the modern academic sense, but as current appropriation and conviction. As Philipse acknowledges in his contribution, but does not seem to take into account in his argumentation: "But the aims of the judge or the cleric are very different from those of the intellectual historian who simply wants to reconstruct the original meaning of obscure passages in old treatises on astronomy, for example."[19] That should be taken into consideration when arguing what view of interpretation is relevant or significant today.

Scalia objects to development in legal interpretation as it does not provide a clear guiding principle. "As soon as the discussion goes beyond the issue of whether the Constitution is static, the evolutionists divide into as many camps as there are individual views of the good, the true, and the beautiful. I think that is inevitably so, which means that evolutionism is simply not a practicable constitutional philosophy."[20] If this were true with respect to the desired flexibility in legal interpretation, this might well be a serious problem as on legal matters in the end some form of social consensus is the aim. But why would such diversity be an issue of concern in religious affairs? What would be the problem, in religious life in a pluralist society, if there is variety according to different conceptions of the good, the true and the beautiful? If religions are about worldviews and values, it is most appropriate that different views of the good, the beautiful and the good correspond to different religious outlooks.

So far, I have accepted that there may be good arguments in favor of the idea that judicial interpretation should stick to the law as far as possible, with limited judicial flexibility, whereas religious interpretation in a living tradition has to allow for reinterpretation in some form in order to be adequate to later experiences and intuitions and relevant in changing circumstances. This difference raises the question how changing circumstances are taken into account in legal interpretation, as legal practice faces new developments and insights as well.

19 Philipse, "Antonin Scalia's Textualism," pp. 30–31.
20 Scalia, *A Matter of Interpretation*, p. 45.

The basic answer seems to me that on law and its development two jobs should be distinguished explicitly. If so, the legal, judicial system is about the application of existing law, whereas the political process is free to set laws, abolish them, change them, and so on. In such a political process, one faces a similar challenge that one faces in religious interpretation, namely, how to combine continuity, which is valuable, with fair consideration of new technologies and situations and with changing moral intuitions. In the legislative process neither originalism nor textualism is appropriate, nor is the neutrality that may be expected of judges in the legal process appropriate here, as making laws is about expressing ideals of a good social order.

If courts and parliaments would function perfectly well, such a division of labor would seem to be a satisfactory combination of two different interests, namely the need for predictability and that for adaptation to changing needs. In practice, the division of labor does not always function as it should. As I see it, it is often the political process that falls short of what it should deliver. Decisions are postponed, or details left are to the legal system as vagueness makes political decisions more smoothly. Especially in the USA, in practice some legislative affairs seem to have been outsourced to the Supreme Court, even though that is not how the role of the court is conceptualized and justified. Whether in parliament or in a court, in a legislative process moral and political pluralism is to be expected and appropriate. It needs to be supplemented by a procedure to decide on a conclusion, for the time being; in a representative democracy most likely by a majority decision of those elected to represent us for some years, after an adequate exchange of considerations and arguments. In this process, originalism is misguided, as this is about convictions shaping society. That is how I understand the suggestion that this is a continuing speech-act, reaffirming and developing the law.

Though roles may be in the same hands, this does not do away with the principle of a difference between the rule of law, as a given, to be applied, that is, to be interpreted with a very moderate amount of flexibility, and the making of law, where neutrality would be nonsensical, as the process is about the framework of values people bring to the process. If a timely revision of laws fails, there may be some license for judicial interpretative flexibility. However, this is business for the philosophers of law, and not for a philosopher of the humanities.

Interpretation is unavoidably human. Law is an important domain, but so, too, is the way we interpret our heritage, and thus articulate our identity. That may involve religious texts and practices, but it may also relate to secular resources, such as national history – whether focusing on the "big names" or on those that have been considered marginal – persons deemed exemplary, a social or political movement one identifies with, or a moral vision. Developing and justifying one's identity by interpreting the resources available, is not a scholarly endeavor but an existential one, something done in living. But it is worthy of critical reflection. Though not a science, it need not be merely haphazard but can be constructive, taking scholarly knowledge into account; an analogy might be engineering, which is itself not a science either, but constructing what one needs for practical purposes – for life as lived, while taking knowledge of materials, design processes and human usage into account.

Though we move beyond the boundaries of the humanities, I conclude with three theses which I hope to have given some plausibility here.

1. Even if there are good reasons for textualism and originalism in legal interpretation and in historical scholarship, these do not carry over to living religion and living law as such are always in process.
2. If we look for an analogy for religious interpretation, we better look at political and legislative processes, involving a person's political preferences, rather than at legal interpretation that aspires to be neutral and predictable.
3. Treating religious traditions, in the absence of a distinction corresponding to the one between political and legal systems, as if they are legal systems, encourages fundamentalist and atheist misunderstandings.

The professional has a task that differs from the role of a scholar. However, professionals can learn from scholars, about the way language was used in the past, about historical contexts in which texts or works of art arose, and more generally about processes of interpretation. To avoid a naïve fundamentalist appropriation of texts, responsible professional interpretations should take into account the scholarship provided by the humanities as far as relevant to the issues at hand.

6

Humans

HUMANITIES ARE ABOUT HUMANS. DONE BY HUMANS. Relevant to humans. Who are we, those humans? We are material beings, we are bodies, always somewhere in space and time. But we are also thinking beings. For many centuries, the basic understanding of humans has been dualist: we are bodies and souls. But our mental life is tied up closely with our physical existence; dualism separates that which is fundamentally intertwined. But if we understand ourselves as material, would it not be enough to study the body – to have just medicine, biology, chemistry, and physics? What is it about humans that evokes the need for a different way of studying each other and ourselves, the humanities?

The natural sciences are about the world out there, but they are also about us. Matter is not a launching pad left behind once we have taken off. At each moment, we are physics, chemistry, and biology at work. As the philosopher John Dewey wrote, stressing the continuity between ordinary experience and experience of art, but so too might one say about human existence and physical reality: [1]

> Mountain peaks do not flow unsupported; they do not even just rest upon the earth. They *are* the earth in one of its manifest operations.

So too for humans, we are material. Thus, by our lives we reveal what matter is capable of.

We are *biological* beings, organisms – matter that has become self-organizing, through a long evolutionary process. In *The Naked Ape*,

1 John Dewey, *Art as Experience* (London: Allen and Unwin, 1934), p. 2.

initially published in 1967, zoologist Desmond Morris treated human behavior in the same way he would have described and explained the behavior of other animals.[2] His discussion of sexual signals, intimacy, the male penis, and the female breasts attracted widespread attention. In the decades since Morris's book came out, sociobiology, evolutionary psychology, and primatology have developed considerably, but the basic message stands: We are apes. As we are such animals, what makes us different from other animals, and even more from yeasts and plants? What would be special about thinking, morality, and culture?

The Naked Ape applies to us, humans. But in our social life, we hardly encounter *naked* apes. We wear clothes. Not just to keep us warm, but also as ways of expressing ourselves. Though we might thus be labelled *dressed* apes, that would suggest that the change is superficial, merely about the way we cover our nakedness. However, culture is not like a dress that covers our naked existence; culture is intrinsic to our human identity. By nature, we are *cultural* and *technological* beings; we are, with words from the philosopher Helmuth Plessner, *artificial by nature*. We have been shaped by biology, culture, and technology, and in the process, we are reshaping our biology, culture, and technology. Biological evolution and historical development have made us *cultural* beings. Our existence today is intertwined with modern technologies. These give us new powers, but are also sources of ambivalence. May we do whatever has become possible? Would that be "playing God?" or merely "human play"?

Even more grandiose: We have become *planetary* beings, interacting with others around the globe, while transforming the surface of our planet, and even its atmosphere and oceans. How should we think of ourselves in light of the ecological challenges that we have created? Do we need a new way of thinking about ourselves, a new cosmic narrative?

In this chapter, we will reflect upon humans, as a way of thinking about the humanities, the disciplines that address most specifically our particular character. We are material, biological, cultural, technological, and planetary beings. How to think of ourselves, as the subjects and objects of the humanities, in the context of this vast universe?

2 Desmond Morris, *The Naked Ape* (London: Jonathan Cape, 1967).

MATERIAL BEINGS

Are we nothing but matter in motion? What about the soul? We have a body, but we are not our bodies. We have a soul, and that is the more significant aspect of human existence. At least, so might argue a dualist. If one were to see humans as consisting of bodies and souls, the need for the humanities as a discipline alongside the natural sciences is obvious, as there would be aspects of human existence not touched upon at all by the natural sciences – the humanities would be the sciences of the soul. Should we thus understand the humanities after their German name, *Geisteswissenschaften*, as the sciences of ghostly aspects of our existence? This would not do justice to the meanings of *Geist*, nor to our constitution.

In 1907 the American Duncan MacDougall published in the journal of the *American Society for Psychical Research* an article that concluded that a human soul weighs about 21 grams. That was the weight loss the moment one dies. He did acknowledge that his research had its limitations. Not in every case, the weight loss happened at the moment of death. Perhaps some souls take longer to leave the body. Besides, measurements had only been successful with four persons, who spent their final hours on a bed positioned on scales. With two others, the measurement failed. One died while MacDougall was still setting up the equipment. Also, with the only woman among his objects of study, others engaged too much with the dying person, thereby disturbing his measurements. For the four for which he presented data, the results were diverse. After a while, two lost more weight; he did not interpret this as evidence for multiple souls. For one, the weight loss was only temporary. The 21 grams was the result of only one measurement. MacDougall reports that for fifteen dogs no weight loss showed up, confirming that dogs don't have a soul. His experiment with the healthy dogs had been much easier, as these had been killed at the moment that suited the researcher.[3]

Most dualists are not such crude materialists about the soul. The greatest dualist of the modern era, the seventeenth century

3 Duncan MacDougal, "Hypothesis Concerning Soul Substance; Together with Experimental Evidence of Such Substance." *Journal of the American Society for Psychical Research* 1 (1907), 237–244.

philosopher René Descartes, considered the physical and the mental to be different substances. Once one assumes such a duality of different elements, the conceptual mystery becomes how the two contributions to human nature work together. As the locus of interaction, Descartes suggested the hypophysis or pituitary gland, deep in the brain, but that suggestion did not help to provide clarity.

Some others have treated the material and the mental as two aspects belonging to a single substance, a dual aspect theory. Spinoza, shortly after Descartes, might be understood thus. Upon such a view, psychology would be more fundamental than physics, as psychology engages both aspects of reality. That does not fit our experience with the sciences, which seem to reflect a rather successful stack of disciplinary levels, from physics via chemistry to biology, and for animals with nerve systems further upwards to neuroscience and psychology. A droplet of water or an electron seems to have no mental pole. A dual aspect view describes the world in our own image, which is convenient but not necessarily correct.

When looking for a distinct entity or property, "the soul," we seem to be misled by language. Nouns often refer to an entity or person: this book, that girl, my house. But there need not be a distinct entity. The philosopher Gilbert Ryle describes in his book *The Concept of Mind* (1949) someone who visits Oxford or Cambridge. They show him the colleges where students live and receive education, libraries, museums, laboratories, offices, and sport facilities. If at the end of the tour, the person complains: "I did not come to see laboratories and libraries; I want to see the university," there is a misunderstanding. The university is not something in addition to labs and libraries, but it is constituted by those facilities and the people working there.[4]

Assume that a ship is in trouble. An SOS message is broadcast; SOS stands for "Save Our Souls." A pious radio operator receives the message, and immediately goes on his knees to pray. Confident about God, he then relays to those on the ship: "Your *souls* have been saved; no further action needed." Was this the response those in fear of drowning, hoped for with the SOS? Didn't they intend that their

4 Gilbert Ryle, *The Concept of Mind* (London: Hutchinson's, 1949), p. 16.

bodies would be saved, and hence their lives? They spoke of "the soul," but they were speaking of living persons, people with bodies.[5]

We are made of water, carbon, phosphorus, while there is iron in the red cells in our blood. If one were to speak in economic terms, the commercial value of a person resides not so much in these materials. Overwhelmingly, it resides in all the labor invested. Labor we do ourselves during all those years of growing up. Labor invested by our parents and teachers. The labor of earlier generations, all those who have created the world we live in, through agriculture and technology, social arrangements, language, and culture. One might even add labor performed by processes in stars long gone, as these processes have created oxygen, carbon, and iron out of hydrogen. There is some fourteen billion years of labor invested in each of us. Processes during those fourteen billion years have made us the complex material beings we are. Thereby, the rich lives we may have, has become possible. But if we are matter organized in complex ways, what about our inner lives? What, to focus on one aspect, about thinking?

If thinking is merely a complex chemical and electrical process going on in our bloody brains, why would it be more significant than digestion, which goes on in our bowels? Material processes go their way; they are not *about* anything. But the sounds we utter when we speak and the markings we scribble on paper when we write, are about something; we write about love, we do arithmetic, we put down on paper how to prepare an apple pie. That is the "about" that humanities deal with. If the conclusion of the scientific view of the world is that brains are complex chemical machines that produce noise mistaken for meaningful words, we seem to be caught in a paradoxical situation, since when we do science, we assume that we are engaging ideas, not merely generating noise. When we understand ourselves as material beings, what would be left of thinking, the significance of words, ideas and symbols, of science and human culture?

A skeptical suspicion seems to follow from the idea that all the work in brains is done by chemical processes. If the current state of the brain

5 The example of the SOS message is inspired by a lecture by the Wittgensteinian philosopher of religion D. Z. Phillips.

corresponds to a particular state of mind, the next state of mind is merely the by-product of the way the brain will be in a fraction of a second from now, and that is a matter of neurotransmitters, not of ideas. Thus, if you are asked to add "23 + 47," and say "70," you would not say 70 because that is the true outcome, but because of the way the brain is wired. All the work seems done by the physical processes, with no real contribution from the meaning of the ideas involved, in this case the numbers and the instruction to add those two numbers. However, in me writing this book, in you reading this book, we are engaged in an exchange of ideas. At least, that is what I aspire to do. Hence, such a material view of human personhood seems insufficient; ideas are more than an irrelevant by-product of the material processes. Do we need a ghost in the machine?

The skeptical suspicion rests upon a false dichotomy, the assumption that the outcome is either due to a materially mediated process *or* that it is driven by the meaning of the notions, in this example the mathematical rules of addition. The confusion arises if one neglects the specifics of the complex physiological process between hearing "23 + 47" and answering "70." The process is a material process, but it is not just any process. We give the answer we give because from the time we started to learn words and numbers, we have been trained to make those connections, and that training prepared the wiring of the brain in the appropriate way. To learn language and symbolic, mathematical thinking, we are engaged in many years of training, training that shapes physiological processes in the brain.

One could make a similar analysis of computers. Under one description, there is nothing but a physical process going on. Upon this description, there is no reason at all to believe that a computer gives a correct answer to the question "23 + 47." If it were to answer "69," there also would have been a physical process in the chips of the computer, and the physics would still hold. However, we expect the computer to reply "70" because that is the correct answer. With computers we have started to use a second level of description, describing it as a machine that deals with numbers (and beyond that, as one that deals with texts, data, and ideas). The crux is that engineers have designed the computer in such a way that the physical process executed corresponds correctly to our expectations regarding the way numbers should be handled. Mathematics – a mental practice – has been guiding a meaningful arrangement of physical processes, processes that taken by themselves are meaningless, just happening.

This parallel of content and process need not be there. Some decades ago, there was a problem with a Pentium chip; some calculations went astray. There was nothing wrong with mathematics, the world of ideas. There was nothing wrong with physics; electrons behaved according to the laws of physics. However, the correspondence between the world of material processes and the meaning we ascribed to the symbols involved was not constructed as it should have been, and thus, the results did not represent what they were supposed to represent.[6]

Back from the computer to humans: Thanks to all the learning that has gone on, embodied in cultural concepts and in actual training, we as material beings can make adequate associations, and hence think adequately. This is not degrading humans; rather, it is upgrading our view of matter. By being constituted the way we are, with all those underlying material processes, we can deal with content, with ideas. But we remain fallible. If we make mistakes, we will start to consider the underlying process. Have I heard you correctly? Or, if it is a more persistent problem, do I really know the meaning of those words? Was I taught well? Or, if the problem is more severe, we sometimes have to conclude, sadly, that the organization is damaged by a tumor or a stroke, incapacitating processes we normally rely upon.

Much more is involved in the reflection upon the relation between the content and process that goes on in our brains; this is the domain of the philosophy of mind, relating a neuroscientific analysis to the mental world. Though there are deep questions, given categorical differences between the mental and the material, a strong dualism of mind and matter would make the relationship between thoughts and actions totally mysterious. But we do not need dualism to argue for meaningful utterances – words and ideas. Material processes in our bodies are organized in such a way that they

6 I owe the example of the Pentium chip to T. Bas Jongeling, "Wat is reductionisme?" in Willem B. Drees (ed.), *De mens: Meer dan materie? Religie en reductionisme* (Kampen: Kok, 1997), 38–54, p. 42; the section on material thinking draws upon Drees, *Religion and Science in Context: A Guide to the Debates* (London: Routledge, 2010), pp. 131–133.

correspond to content, and in that sense those processes can be analyzed in terms of their meaning.

BIOLOGICAL BEINGS

We are the realization of a particular possibility of nature, the possibility of personal existence. In between the material and the personal, there is the biological – we are living beings, heirs of a long evolutionary history.

Important to my understanding of the humanities are two fertile features of the biological process: The *diversities* it generates and the role of *circularities* throughout the process. Biology generates diversity. Many life forms co-exist. Each individual is different, due to minor variations in the genetic and environmental legacy involved. Biology is evolutionary history. In the course of time, many thresholds have been passed. Such historical transitions cannot be undone easily; once we have learned to do something, it is hard to undo it – just as it is hard to forget once one knows something. Once hominids mastered fire, made tools, and communicated through language, their inventions became a given for later generations. Over time the legacy became more complex, and thereby the possibilities for further forms of diversity. What does such an evolutionary perspective imply, for us, for culture, for morality?

Can human morality, the practice of making moral judgments, be understood as a fruit of human evolution, of the way we have come to be who we are? Hardly anyone objects when an evolutionary approach would be invoked to explain in humans the almost complete loss of fur. But can morality be explained evolutionarily? How could morality have arisen through evolution, since evolution favors self-interest, whereas moral behavior is to the benefit of others? Also, if morality would be evolutionary explainable, should we consider it really moral? Or does morality require something categorically different?[7]

Let us begin with close kin. Taking care of children, nephews, and nieces is evolutionarily intelligible as it serves genetic self-interest.

7 Drees, *Religion, Science and Naturalism* (Cambridge University Press, 1996), pp. 199–221.

Genes that promote social behavior within the family promote the spread of copies of themselves in the next generation. Support of one's partner is also evolutionarily intelligible too since the shared investment in children implies common interests. Also, for beings with a reasonable memory, helping one's neighbor is evolutionarily intelligible as well, as in an indefinite future I might have to ask my neighbor for help. Helping a stranger might perhaps be understood as an example of "indirect reciprocity." By displaying pro-social behavior my status among friends and neighbors rises, and this could pay off.

There may also be explanations in terms of the collective interest of my tribe, village, or nation. By doing something for my village, we may thrive in the competition with other villages. By serving my group, even if this includes more than my relatives, my children will benefit as well. Such an explanation allows for a cynical aside: We benefit even more when we invest less in the common cause than it appears, as we individually may profit from the benefits that befall on our group without sharing the burden as much as the others do. The evolution of deception is, upon this view, intertwined with the evolution of social behavior; free riding is a recurrent concern. With the evolution of deception, also the evolution of our ability to spot deception; it is an arms race. Holding up ideals about pro-social behavior, an emerging moral ideology, may be beneficial as well, as it makes the others more likely to help the group, and hence me. Ideas along lines as indicated here may do the job of explaining pro-social behavior among humans quite well, while also explaining that we do not always live up to it.

Is such pro-social behavior merely a pragmatic issue, as it works for those involved? Can moral *arguments* be justified, and not merely be explained? Criteria that figure in justification, such as disinterestedness and universalizability may be understood in the context of our evolutionary past. Perhaps, one day one of our predecessors was asked by another human, or hominid, something equivalent to: "Why did you do that?" Others may have been present. If so, referring to one's own emotions would not serve well as an answer, nor would do an appeal to self-interest. The justification of one's behavior would have to be relevant to all present. Thus, one might see a beginning of moral considerations that surpass self-interest.

In Amsterdam, tall but narrow houses and warehouses along the canals have hooks, used to haul up spices, coffee, tea, and other products from colonial trade – and nowadays to haul up furniture for expensive apartments. The hooks are part of the house that has been built from the ground up. There are no hooks that come down from the sky, without an earthly base. As an alternative to imaginary sky hooks, the philosopher Daniel Dennett used the image of cranes. Large cranes can be built up with smaller cranes; there are no miracles involved in the process upwards. So, too, in the history of technology: with primitive tools, somewhat more advanced tools were made, and with these even more advanced tools. So, too, in the history of knowledge; knowledge allows us to develop further knowledge, to extend and revise our earlier ideas. So, too, for social arrangements and moral convictions; they may have been improved step by step, piecemeal wise, by solving problems as they arose, on the go. This trajectory sketches a pragmatic explanatory approach such as the one developed by Philip Kitcher in *The Ethical Project*.[8]

But if moral behavior is evolutionarily intelligible, would it not be dishonest, covering the lowlier reality of self-interested behavior? I do not think so. We withdraw our hand from a flame. Those who did not do so, became handicapped or might even die from infections. Hence, they produced children less often or were less able to protect and support them. However, upon the question "Why do you withdraw your hand?" the response is not, "In order to have more children," but "Because it hurts." That the sensibility to pain and the reflex to withdraw has an evolutionary explanation, does not make the pain less real or the verbal explication dishonest.

So, too, for morality: The existence of an evolutionary explanation for pro-social behavior need not imply that we are not driven by genuine moral considerations and sentiments. Rather, becoming humans, with moral sentiments and reflection, has been the way in which a fruitful social life has become possible. There is no reason to deny the genuineness of human culture and moral convictions because

8 Daniel Dennett, *Darwin's Dangerous Idea: Evolution and the Meanings of Life* (New York: Simon & Schuster, 1995); Philip Kitcher, *The Ethical Project* (Cambridge, MA: Harvard University Press, 2011).

of their origins in our evolutionary history. Ethical objectivity need not be linked to a realm of ethereal entities, such as abstract values. Values have been invented, as humans needed to refer to a shared standard, a standard in which the interests of others are taken into account as well. In this process, not only the standards may have become more universal, but the circle of morally relevant persons also may have expanded. Thus, moral reasoning may have emerged and developed. This is similar to a pragmatic understanding of mathematics; one might see it as rooted in practices such as counting and measuring, over time learning that it is possible to abstract from apples, pears, and oranges, to articulate general insights about numbers and geometry.

The ability to engage in abstract forms of reflection, which allows us to distance ourselves somewhat from immediate inclinations, is itself a natural capacity. It may have served other functions in our evolutionary past; thinking allows for flexible responses to changing circumstances and anticipatory thinking may considerably diminish risks. Whatever the origin of the human capacity for reflection on one's own behavior and the behavior of others, we now have this capacity and can use it for new purposes, such as a reconsideration of our moral intuitions and judgments. This human capacity for reasoning, and the patterns of reasoning which we are able to pursue, is subject to development as well.

Formal analysis, the application of criteria such as disinterestedness and coherence, and the moral deliberation of many people together are important for the credibility of morality, precisely because we thereby may surpass and correct the conclusions of our ordinary biological and psychological mechanisms. To *justify* the validity of moral norms, one might argue along Kantian lines, justifying values via the conditions for human agency or judgment. Though morality is made by humans, it may categorically transcend us in its aspirations.[9]

Evolution has delivered more than was ordered. Means can be used for new purposes. Our ten fingers did not evolve to play a piano, but they can be used to play the piano. In evolutionary history new uses of old organs can be found again and again. Intelligence and

9 Sem de Maagt, *Constructing Morality: Transcendental Arguments in Ethics* (PhD thesis, Utrecht University, 2017).

communication, brains and language will have been useful for the four essential Fs: feeding, fighting, fleeing, and reproducing. Once intelligence and language evolved, they may have been used in other tasks as well. The more that was delivered allows morality to be genuinely moral, for our intelligence allows us to reconsider our own behavior. For instance, we may discover that we are naturally inclined to treat men and women differently. By becoming aware of this we can also act against apparently self-evident natural inclinations. The social context of our lives may have pushed us toward universality and accountability, hallmarks of morality.

Sometimes, we are open to reasons, to argument. Since ideas spread faster than genes, as genes are transferred only to one's own offspring while ideas may spread in many ways, culture may develop enormously. There is no reason to assume that the biological basis would always overrule the effects of culture. Thanks to the emergence of culture as a second kind of heritage, alongside the genetic one, and thanks to the capacity for reflection and to the impulse to public justification, we are not victims of our evolutionary heritage. We are biological beings, but as these particular biological beings we have a moderate amount of freedom with respect to our genetic drives. We therefore also have responsibility.

Organisms not only adapt to their given environment; they also reshape their environment and thus construct niches which may suit them better. *Circularity* is abundant in the natural world, beginning with the chemistry of DNA and proteins, if not much earlier. In logic, self-reference may be fatal, as in a phrase like "This sentence is false." If the sentence is false, it is true. But if it is true, it is false. Circularity may be powerless, as in the case of the fictitious Baron Munchhausen who claimed to have extracted himself from a moor by pulling himself up by his bootstraps. In reality, however, recursion and self-reference may be enormously powerful, an ascending spiral. *Gödel, Escher, Bach*, the title of a book by Douglas Hofstadter, refers to three major figures who have shown the power of recursion and self-reference in logic, in graphic arts, and in musical compositions.[10]

10 Douglas R. Hofstadter, *Gödel, Escher, Bach: An Eternal Golden Braid* (New York: Basic Books, 1979).

Hofstadter's book expresses in imagery shaped by logic and technology the philosophical anthropology offered by Helmuth Plessner in his work *The Levels of Organic Life and the Human*, originally *Die Stufen des Organischen und der Mensch* (1928). Plessner introduces his own conceptual language to speak of the particular richness of the human experience of the world, and with that of human agency, as a possibility within natural reality. Plessner relates explicitly to Wilhelm Dilthey, whom we encountered above as a founding figure of the *Geisteswissenschaften*, the humanities. Thus, it is no coincidence that his anthropology relates the biological perspective to a humanities perspective.

As a first step, one might say that each living organism is characterized by a metabolism, taking food in and pushing waste out, and with that by a permeable boundary between inside and outside. Thus, with life there arises an inner world, while the organism is also within its outer world, its environment. Hence, the organism has a particular place in the world; *positionality* becomes a characteristic of life. This works out differently for different kinds of organisms. Schematically, Plessner distinguishes plants, animals, and humans. Plants have no center that coordinates actions, and hence no relationship to their own positionality. Animals are aware of their environment and their own position in it. As they move around, they engage in intentional action; they have a *centric* positionality. Thus, for an animal one might say that it has a body, while it also is that body.

With humans, a further step is made with the emergence of *self*-awareness, awareness of one's own center, and of the possibility that one could have been at a different place or time. In the words of Plessner, "*Er lebt und erlebt nicht nur, sondern er erlebt sein Erleben*" – "He not only lives and experiences, but also experiences himself experiencing."[11] Thus, in our experiences we may take distance from our own center, which thus might also be "looked at" as if from outside that center. Thus, one can want to be more one's true self – as if at any

11 Helmut Plessner, *Die Stufen des Organischen und der Mensch: Einleitung in die philosophische Anthropologie*, originally 1928, reprinted in *Gesammelte Schriften IV* (Frankfurt am Main: Suhrkamp, 1981); quote from p. 364. Translated by Millay Hyatt as: Plessner, *The Levels of Organic Life and the Human: An Introduction to Philosophical Anthropology* (New York: Fordham University Press, 2019), p. 271.

moment one is not one's self. Plessner speaks of persons as having an *ex-centric* positionality, given their ability to engage in self-reflection, to consider their own actions as if from an external perspective. And in this self-reflective process as ex-centric beings, we also encounter others, and hence participate in a shared historical, cultural, and social world (*Mitwelt*). We are products of this shared world that precedes us and shapes us, but we are also its creators. Being a person, an actor in the world, we have practical self-understanding. We realize ourselves through culture, including technology. This is immediately relevant for our topic: As Jos de Mul wrote:

> Although our excentric positionality excludes that we will ever reach a final home, it also incites us to one of the most wonderful journeys a species ever undertook. To reflect and interpret the history of this journey is one of the honorable tasks of the humanities.[12]

Plessner's imagery and language, is just one conceptual vocabulary for philosophical anthropology; others have done it differently. In whatever way human evolution is described, over time, with innumerable transitions, organized matter has become, among much else, Mozart, Einstein, Jesus, Buddha – and each of us.[13] Such a naturalistic view of us is not one that downgrades humans. Rather, it should make us appreciate the rich possibilities of nature.

CULTURAL BEINGS

We are cultural beings. Culture has made us the beings we are. We have remarkable brains and vocal cords because these biological adaptations were selected for by the social and cultural demands of earlier hominid existence. The flexibility of our hands, our prolonged infancy, and capacities for learning: Adaptations such as these make culture possible, but they are also consequences of the cultural needs of our ancestors. We are the product of circularity, or rather of the fertile

12 Jos De Mul, "The Emergence of Practical Self-Understanding: Human Agency and Downward Causation in Plessner's Philosophical Anthropology." *Human Studies* 42 (2019), 65–82, p. 81.

13 "Matter becoming Mozart," is inspired by Arthur R. Peacocke; see his early *Science and the Christian Experiment* (Oxford University Press, 1971), p. 105, and later writings.

spiral of bio-cultural evolution. In our bodies and our brains, we are cultural.

We humans can form images of the world, and of ourselves in this world, and present those to others and to ourselves. Language is a major example of circularity: I am using language to write about language. With *language*, more possibilities have opened up, as language allows for imagination, for making present to others and to ourselves what is not real. With language, we can transcend our immediate situation, with memories of the past and plans for the future.[14]

A plurality of worldviews, religious and secular, is typical of humans as cultural beings. A worldview brings together models *of* the world and models *for* the world, ideas about what there is and about what we would like to exist.[15] Persistent disagreements may involve worldviews and political agendas. As humans we have to live with such a diversity of perspectives and interests, and thus need to promote a civil and democratic process that allows the plurality of voices to be heard. *Convergence* has arisen in some domains. Within groups, moral codes take precedence over individual interests. From counting and measuring we have created mathematics, which in its abstraction goes far beyond the particular circumstances of any time, place, or language. In the natural sciences, with generalizations, the testing of theories about underlying mechanisms, and the intentional effort to reduce the impact of non-epistemic values, we have discovered knowledge that transcends cultural diversity, even though the reception of such insights is highly diverse, loaded with various preferences.

Is there also cultural convergence? Have different cultures had similar developments, also in periods when globalization was not yet such a pervasive phenomenon? Deep down in the evolution of humanity, we go back to shared roots anyhow, as our ancestors all came out of Africa. But here, the question is about more recent cultural developments such as the rise of religions with moral codes, where persons

14 Terrence Deacon, *The Symbolic Species: The Co-Evolution of Language and the Human Brain* (New York: Norton, 1997).

15 Drawing on the definition of religion by Clifford Geertz in "Religion as a Cultural System," in Geertz, *The Interpretation of Cultures* (New York: Basic Books, 1973), 87–125.

are deemed to be of value individually, and not merely as members of group. Some think that such a shared origin of major features of human culture would help overcome divisions that are unjust, as in racism.

Karen Armstrong, a popular writer on religion, is concerned about human aggression, nuclear weapons, ecological damage, and the loss of respect for humans. These issues need more than rational and pragmatic consideration; we need to become engaged. But there is hope.

> In our current predicament, I believe that we can find inspiration in the period that the German philosopher Karl Jaspers called the Axial Age because it was pivotal to the spiritual development of humanity. From about 900 to 200 BCE, in four distinct regions, the great world traditions that have continued to nourish human beings have come into being: Confucianism and Daoism in China; Hinduism and Buddhism in India; monotheism in Israel; and philosophical rationalism in Greece. This was the period of the Buddha, Socrates, Confucius, and Jeremiah, the mystics of the Upanishads, Mencius, and Euripides. During this period of intense creativity, spiritual and philosophical geniuses pioneered an entirely new kind of human experience.

The traditions that arose in this period "pushed forward the frontiers of human consciousness and discovered a transcendent dimension in the core of their being." "The Axial peoples all found that the compassionate ethic worked."[16]

For John Hick, prominent philosopher of religion, the concept of an Axial Age provided a basis for his view of religions as equally respectable moral and affective human responses to the transcendent – at least, so he holds for the post-Axial religions.

> In all these forms the ultimate, the divine, the Real, is that which makes possible a transformation of our present existence, whether by being drawn into fellowship with the transcendent Thou, or by realizing our deeper self as one with the Real, or by unlearning our habitual ego-centredness and becoming a conscious and accepting part of the endless flow of life which is both *saṃsāra* and *nirvana*.[17]

16 Karen Armstrong, *The Great Transformation: The Origin of Our Religious Traditions* (New York: Alfred A. Knopf, 2006), pp. xi–xiv.

17 John Hick, *An Interpretation of Religion: Human Responses to the Transcendent* (Houndmills, Basingstoke: Macmillan, 1989), p. 33.

The idea that there has been an Axial Age or, in the original German, *Achsenzeit,* plays a role as well in other wide ranging approaches to religion, to understand its history and the history of civilizations and possibilities for religion in our time.[18]

Concerning the Axial Age, I have two questions. One is a scholarly one: Has there been such a period, as a coherent phenomenon? The other is about appropriation: Is this a helpful concept for our time? Does it undergird the moral and religious messages that some of its advocates derive from this way of understanding human history? Let us first consider whether this is a fair description of history.

In his *Convenient Myths: The Axial Age, Dark Green Religion, and the World That Never Was*, Iain Provan doubts that it is. In the period just following the Second World War, Karl Jaspers "was concerned to identify something that modern human beings hold in common – something that might unify humanity and help us all to move forward together peaceably. He believed he had discovered what was needed, not in any single religious or philosophical system, but in a specific historical experience: the axial age." But a perceived need does not make it true.[19]

Scholars might ask whether some of the changes regarded typical for this period may already be discerned in cultures or periods labelled pre-axial.[20] Is the scheme not excessively imposing a systematic distinction on pre-axial, axial and post-axial cultures? Are we looking at

18 Shmuel Eisenstadt, *The Origins and Diversity of Axial Age Civilizations* (Albany, NY: State University of New York Press, 1986); Johann P. Arnason, S. N. Eisenstadt and Björn Wittrock (eds.), *Axial Civilizations and World History* (Leiden: Brill, 2005); Robert N. Bellah, *Religion in Human Evolution: From the Paleolithic to the Axial Age* (Cambridge, MA: Harvard University Press, 2011); Robert N. Bellah and Hans Joas (eds.), *The Axial Age and Its Consequences* (Cambridge, MA: Harvard University Press, 2012); Joas, *Die Macht des Heiligen. Eine Alternative zur Geschichte von der Entzauberung* (Berlin: Suhrkamp, 2017).

19 Iain Provan, 2013. *Convenient Myths: The Axial Age, Dark Green Religion, and the World that Never Was* (Waco, TX: Baylor University Press, 2013), p. 2, refers to Karl Jaspers, *The Origin and Goal of History* (London: Routledge & Kegan Paul, 1953), p. 19.

20 Christoph Harbsmeier, "The Axial Millennium in China: A Brief Survey," in *Axial Civilizations and World History*, 469–507; Eisenstadt, "Axial Civilizations and the Axial Age Reconsidered," in *Axial Civilizations and World History*, 531–564; Arnason, "The Axial Age and Its Interpreters: Reopening a Debate," in *Axial Civilizations and World History*, 19–49; Arnason, "Rehistoricizing the Axial Age," in *The Axial Age and Its Consequences*, 337–365.

the relevant period, or should we rather take a different era or millennium? Another scholar suggested taking the first millennium CE, thus including the development of Buddhism in China, Christianity in the West, and the emergence of Islam. The image of an axis around which everything rotates is already somewhat problematic when that axial age is taken to extend over many centuries. What happened at different places is characterized as much by differences as by similarities. Thus, many scholars who use the terminology, have come to acknowledge its limitations and thus its modest status as an interpretation of a rich variety of the cultural changes that occurred in a particular period.

Karen Armstrong uses the idea that there has been an Axial Age to support a spiritual and moral message for our time. Her plea for compassion is laudable, but such a useful image of the past seems too convenient. The past is different, and not necessarily supportive of our ideals. It seems that historical scholarship does not deliver a coherent Axial Age, but even if it would, it is implausible that it would provide a message for our time, given vastly different conditions, with shifts from agriculture to cities, from philosophy to science and technology, and with globalization at a planetary scale. Existentially relevant interpretations of the past may be meaningful, but those are to be distinguished from careful scholarship. Even authors who are more scholarly, and hence hedge their reference to the axial period in various ways, may claim too much coherence by using this label. On Robert Bellah's book *Religion in Human Evolution*, Provan observes that the more attention Bellah gives to each of the cultures individually, the more the idea of a coherent Axial Age seems to lose meaning.

There are two different reasons why it might be deemed problematical to use the concept of an Axial Age, or any other such historical claim, if it were to do justice to our knowledge of those periods. The first one mentioned by Provan is moral; projecting upon people of an earlier time an idea that is not adequate, does violence to those cultures, with their religions and philosophies.

> It seems to me that such avoidance of violence matters. We ought, I think, to try to treat our neighbors in the past just as well as we try to treat them in the present. We ought not to misrepresent them, we ought to try to understand what they mean and not twist their words, and we ought not simply to use them in pursuit of our own agendas.

> These are ethical imperatives that many people try to live by in the present. I do not see why they should not apply to the past as well.

The second concern is more pragmatic: Distortions

> matter because the past, the present, and the future are so closely bound up with each other. (. . .) If I do not get the story straight with respect to the past – if I start believing claims about the past that are simply not true – then there is a very good chance that I will make significant mistakes in my thinking and living in the present.[21]

But one might take the Axial Age view of history not as a story about the past but as a heuristic tool, a frame that we bring to the material, to highlight some aspects of the past and thereby help us see some aspects of that life world that we might otherwise miss and, again, may inspire us in our own lives.[22] Or we might understand Karen Armstrong's historical narrative as a moral injunction – to become like this imagined past. But that would not be a scholarly approach, though appropriation of history is human.

Scholarship is important, to be honest to those studied, whether people from a distant past or fellow humans with a different way of life. Drawing on such scholarship for our own orientation in life has, however, its risks, as we might use it in ways shaped more by our interests than by respect for the ideas and practices of those others.

TECHNOLOGICAL BEINGS

As cultural beings, we have become *technological* beings. Technology is culture and it changes culture. Our identities and responsibilities, the communities we belong to, our attitudes, hopes, dreams, and nightmares are shaped by rapidly evolving technology. Antibiotics and sewage systems have changed our vulnerability. Contraceptives have changed relations between men and women, and hence between parents and their sons and daughters. The Internet has changed the

21 Provan, *Convenient Myths*, pp. 107f., 122 and 19.

22 Heiner Roetz, *Confucian Ethics of the Axial Age: A Reconstruction under the Aspect of the Breakthrough toward Postconventional Thinking* (Albany, NY: State University of New York Press, 1993), who in the title of his third chapter speaks of a "Universalistic Heuristic of Enlightenment."

nature of information and communication. Technology does not offer us entrance into a different world, such as the metaphor of "cyberspace" suggested, but it has made our world different, and will continue to do so.

The way digital technologies transform culture, including the way we express ourselves in rituals, narratives, and art, is a topic for cultural studies, while the ways in which technology mediated communication changes our behavior is a typical topic for communication sciences. Technology changes us and our cultural social world. We are *artificial by nature*, to evoke a phrase by Helmuth Plessner; the uneasiness of the eccentric position is made up for by creating a particular human world to live in, that is, the world of technology and culture.[23]

We even use technological images to speak about ourselves and our experiences. Ever needed "to blow off steam"? The metaphor is still alive, even though steam engines are a distant past. Who has never experienced "stress" or been under "huge pressure"? Not only our self-image and self-understanding have been influenced by technology but so have our lives. We have outsourced aspects of human existence, and in doing so our understanding of humanity has changed. With *tools* we still had to provide power, but could do things that we would not be able to do with our bare hands. Alongside tools, we also see the development of the telescope and the microscope, *instruments* that have extended our observational abilities, especially since the seventeenth century.

Harnessing sources of power, whether those of wind, water, and animals, or those of steam engines and internal combustion, has allowed us to let *machines* do substantial physical labor. Machines need human control, partially realized via feedback loops, such as the thermostat to control temperature. The Industrial Age of the eighteenth and nineteenth century coincided with the rise of modern science, understanding reality as lawful. What in an earlier stage was left implicit as knowledge of skilled persons, has now been analyzed so that it could be implemented in a process done by machines and

23 "Artificial by nature" is the first of Plessner's anthropological laws (*Die Stufen*, Chapter 7.3); De Mul, "Artificial by Nature: An Introduction to Plessner's Philosophical Anthropology," in Jos de Mul (ed.), *Plessner's Philosophical Anthropology: Perspectives and Prospects* (Amsterdam University Press, 2016), 11–37.

workers. Production is depersonalized, relative to the earlier stage when it was more a personal skill, an art.

While in the Industrial Age we outsourced power, modern *information* technologies have allowed us to move further in objectifying and outsourcing processes. Chess may be a typical example, symbolized by the 1997 match of world champion Garry Kasparov and Deep Blue II, won by the computer, or one might say, more appropriately, by the human team that developed the computer. Other tasks such as face recognition and automatic translation turned out to be harder, as there is more ambiguity and context dependence in language and social interactions, but in recent years newly developed technologies have become better at such tasks. The variation and confusion that can be handled automatically has increased, as analytical skills and learning abilities have been objectified too. Thus, much that used to be "typically human" has gradually been objectified and outsourced, and thereby modified, extended, and improved.[24]

People are ambivalent about new technologies. Much is taken for granted, and even more is expected or feared. A recent dystopian novel is *The Circle* by Dave Eggers. A young woman lands the job she dreams of at The Circle, the world's most powerful Internet company, at their headquarters in Silicon Valley. The company seeks to use all the data it collects for good causes, for instance to return abducted children to their parents and to promote transparency in politics. One quiet evening she takes a kayak out onto the Bay, she sees seals and enjoys the quietness of the night. In the world of massive data her escape does not go unnoticed. She should not have kept this experience to herself; handicapped persons might have enjoyed sharing her experience. One of the slogans she invents for the company is PRIVACY IS THEFT. An interesting use of language. The young woman goes "fully transparent," so that people can follow her activities via the web, and thousands do, and later millions. Politicians come under pressure to go fully transparent too. Soon, all information will

24 Tools, machines, information processing: Maarten Coolen, *De machine voorbij: Over het zelfbegrip van de mens in het tijdperk van de informatietechniek* (Meppel: Boom, 1992).

become readily available to all, everything will be transparent, which will make for a perfect world.

Earlier I spoke of "circularity." In the words the novel attributes to leaders of the company, "the circle will close." Everything will become available as data. But the circle cannot close. The company itself is not fully transparent. It is impossible that the company ever could be. A map of reality that is as complete as reality itself cannot exist, as part of the reality the map intends to depict in full detail is the map itself. In the context of the novel: The machines where the data are processed are not on the map.[25]

In dealing with ourselves as biological, cultural, and technological beings, with our powers as actors in constructing further technology and living with the technologies that we have constructed, there is much to be studied and reflected upon. We must consider critical questions. Do these technologies facilitate extreme forms of surveillance and centralized control? Who profits and who suffers from adverse consequences? However, it is impossible to close the circle, to have final and complete knowledge. There is a human potential for creativity and wisdom, precisely because of the possibility of self-reflection, of a circularity that takes the form of a spiral rather than a circle that would bring one back to the same point again and again.

There are genuine challenges that require reflection. With new powers, we need to become wiser, we need to become *techno sapiens*. From *homo sapiens*, the naked ape, to techno sapiens: We are biological and technological, in a globalizing, data-driven world. Whether we are wise, this being the meaning of the Latin designation *sapiens*, remains to be seen, but at least it is something we should aspire to be.

We are not merely shaped by technology; we are its creators as well. The powers we have acquired may give rise to an unnerving question: Are we overstepping a boundary? Are we "playing God?" Accusing someone of "playing God" may occur in two different contexts. The traditional meaning can be illustrated by concerns one may have about the death penalty: Is it up to us to decide on issues of life and death? There is no doubt that we, humans, always have been able to kill other

25 Dave Eggers, *The Circle* (New York: Knopf and San Francisco: McSweeney, 2013), p. 219ff.

humans. The grave question is whether we consider the use of these powers justifiable.

The question whether we overstep a boundary arises in a rather different way when we acquire new powers, for instance when selecting embryos or modifying genes. Issues that used to be non-moral now have come within our domain of responsibility. The image of a boundary is helpful, as a boundary between two domains, distinguishing that which is beyond our control, which is "a given," and that which is our responsibility. With the acquisition of new powers processes or circumstances that once were accepted as if due to fate, may now be modified intentionally. The boundary moves. Never before was it up to us to make those particular decisions, for instance about the genetic make-up of the next generation. Thus, we need to create criteria for morally acceptable actions. Nervousness about "playing God" may well concern moral, political, and legal issues that arise when the boundary shifts. We have to address issues that were never within our powers before, and with which we have no experience yet. New powers may require new moral principles or, less revolutionary, new ways of applying existing fundamental principles. In a broader anthropological sense, this dynamic is part of what it is to be human – it is "playing human."[26]

Given the co-evolution of biology and culture, living with a shifting boundary is nothing new. Living with structural change is unavoidably part of the human condition, it is part of the spiral of being conditioned while at the same time shaping the conditions. We are at the same time products of the past and actors in the present. Also, humans are *self*-reflective, they think about their world and their own actions, and about their own thinking about their world and actions.

PLANETARY BEINGS

Not only are we living with others, locally. Humanity is present almost everywhere, with global impact. Ours is not the first time that biological beings reshape the planet. The oxygen rich atmosphere is due to biological activity of single cell organisms. Even from a distance, the

26 Ronald Dworkin, *Sovereign Virtue: The Theory and Practice of Inequality* (Cambridge, MA: Harvard University Press, 2000), pp. 442–446.

atmosphere reveals the Earth as a planet with life. Life itself is a planetary phenomenon.

With globalization, human life has become a planetary phenomenon, too. Travel, trade, communication: Many of our activities now span the globe. Culturally, one might speak of globalization, as fashion, movies, and much else that have arisen in one place may be appropriated in other places. But globalization does not imply homogeneity. As Arjun Appadurai wrote, "globalization is itself a deeply historical, uneven, and even *localizing* process. Globalization does not necessarily or even frequently imply homogenization or Americanization, and to the extent that different societies appropriate the material of modernity differently, there is still ample room for the deep study of specific geographies, histories, and languages."[27] With the penchant for inventing new words, some scholars have come to speak of *glocalization*, as the way elements from this global exchange of goods and ideas are used in various places varies highly with local context. Some such variation may be accidental, for instance in the way the pronunciation of English is influenced by a particular mother tongue. But glocalization is often intentional, a selective way of adapting and appropriating global trends to reflect and express particular identities.

The human impact on Earth is such that some even have come to speak of the *Anthropocene* as a new geological epoch. Physically, this might be characterized by the global presence of traces of plastics and of nuclear tests in the decades after World War II, but perhaps one should go back a few more centuries and consider the impact of the Industrial Revolution, or even take into account the millennia of agriculture, or, a still larger temporal span though geologically still rather short, the millennia since hunter-gatherers changed the landscape with fire while hunting various species of big mammals and birds into extinction. Not only on Earth have humans left discernible traces; a few of us have also left footsteps on the Moon and equipment on Mars. With space travel, we have seen the Earth from a distance, resulting in new iconic images, the Earth rising over the moon's surface (December 24, 1968) and the Earth as a pale blue dot seen from afar (1990). Though space travel is driven by national prestige

27 Arjun Appadurai, *Modernity at Large: Cultural Dimensions of Globalization* (Minneapolis: Public Worlds, 1996), p. 17.

and military interests, it also has become a context in which people have emphasized humanity as a collective and the planet as "our home."

In 2012, the John W. Kluge Center at the Library of Congress, Washington DC, in partnership with the NASA Astrobiology Institute, advertised a chair in astrobiology, to pursue "research at the intersection of the science of astrobiology and its humanistic and societal implications." The first person appointed to this chair, David Grinspoon, wrote *Earth in Human Hands: Shaping Our Planet's Future.* Grinspoon argues that whereas our planetary impact, such as the emission of greenhouse gases as a by-product of the Industrial Revolution, modern agriculture, and transport, has been unintentional, we now have to become intentional about such actions, and take our responsibility. There is at least one positive example: Humanity responded to discoveries regarding the hole in the ozone layer, growing due to gasses used in refrigerators. The problem was addressed in agreements in Vienna (1988) and Montreal (1989). Ending the use of those gases was relatively easy, as an alternative already had been developed and patented, by the same company that profited from the earlier gasses. Thus, the change did not upset commercial or national interests too much.[28]

"We" have become a planetary force. But who are "we"? Humanity. People with a variety of interests and concerns. Some have "a seat at the table," or at least might consider themselves represented, while interests of others are hardly taken into account. Thus, planetary developments such as climate change, and the need for an adequate human response, have become major areas of cultural and political controversy.

Also, as with pluralism in the social sphere, we see various proposals on the best way to stimulate morally responsible action. In line with

28 David Grinspoon, *Earth in Human Hands: Shaping Our Planet's Future* (New York: Grand Central Publishing, 2016), p. xi. "Life as a planetary phenomenon" was a key notion in research groups during the Princeton based Center of Theological Inquiry's three years study on "the societal implications of astrobiology," 2015–2018. "Earthrise" is a picture made on December 24, 1968 on the Apollo 8 mission. "Pale Blue Dot" is the name of a photograph made by the Viking I space probe on February 14, 1990, looking back from forty times the distance Earth–Sun.

photographs such as Earth Rise and Pale Blue Dot, some authors stress how much we are together in this. One example is *Journey of the Universe*, a film and multimedia project overseen by Mary Evelyn Tucker, a religious studies scholar, and evolutionary cosmologist Brian Swimme. They present scientific information in the form of a grand evolutionary narrative, weaving together scientific knowledge and humanistic concerns, thereby seeking to evoke wonder and a sense of connectedness and responsibility. In doing so, they see this as a science-based creation story for our time, similar to the way the various world religions offer narratives that may help us understand ourselves and frame our responsibility.

The turn toward a new cosmology akin to religious creation stories has been challenged by Lisa Sideris in her book *Consecrating Science: Wonder, Knowledge and the Natural World.* Whereas in the new grand narratives wonder seems to be mediated by scientific knowledge, Sideris prefers to envisage wonder as rooted in more immediate personal experiences. The grand narrative becomes itself one of the available narratives, alongside others, rather than the narrative shared by all. As Sideris sees it, Tucker seeks to "tell a convincing story" as people want big stories, but in that role, she goes beyond the boundaries of scholarship to become an advocate, though she draws on her knowledge, on science and on the world religions to offer myths and metaphors, images and poetry that may inspire to promote ecological consciousness. In contrast to such a use of human traditions as resources, Sideris positions the humanities as critical discourse, as posing questions, challenging the visionary discourse, the engagement for a higher cause. This is a critical engagement that is also typical of the humanities.[29]

A cosmic narrative offers a grand narrative that gives unity and orientation. In doing so, a motivational, moral message is aligned with a claim about the way things have come to be the way they are. The combination, if used as an argumentative structure, is philosophically

29 Lisa H. Sideris, *Consecrating Science: Wonder, Knowledge, and the Natural World* (Oakland: University of California Press, 2017); Mary Evelyn Tucker, "*Journey of the Universe:* Weaving Science with the Humanities." *Zygon: Journal of Religion and Science* 54 (2019), 409–425; Sideris, "Wonder Sustained: A Reply to Critics." *Zygon: Journal of Religion and Science* 54 (2019), 426–453.

problematical; transitioning from a descriptive analysis to a moral injunction is called by philosophers the "naturalistic fallacy." That particular cosmetics are "natural," does not make them automatically healthy; that certain practices might be "unnatural" does not make these morally wrong, and so too for all transitions from "what is" to "what ought to be." But In religious discourse, models *of* the world and models *for* the world are intertwined; creation stories deal with origins but also provide normative orientation. As long as such stories are recognized as similar to religious discourse, rather than as scholarship, this may be fine, even though it goes beyond the sciences and the humanities. Humans live by more than by humanities and science alone.

Though there is much else besides the humanities, the humanities are characteristic of human existence. As biocultural beings, creating our world with language and technology, we also need to look in the mirror, reflect upon our lives and our actions. Not because there is an absolute boundary between what is given to us and what is up to us, a boundary that we would transgress when playing God. We rather need to reflect upon our lives and actions because there is no such boundary. In human play, we need to consider again and again in which direction we will go forward, whether we will transgress current boundaries, and how, when, and where we will do so, and to the benefit of whom. A salient feature of the humanities in this context is to be alert to human diversity, to conceptual questions, to rhetoric, the language used to convince people, to justification, the arguments that might be deemed valid. Humanities are critical human self-reflection.

7

The Value of the Humanities

THE HUMANITIES ARE CONSIDERED HERE AS THE systematic effort to understand and evaluate human understanding of ourselves, of fellow humans, and of the social and cultural world we create together. Such a program includes the quest for sound knowledge of particulars and of general patterns, sensitivity to the linguistic and situational challenges that come with any effort to understand others, the hermeneutical interest in dialogue, and the challenge to justify one's own judgements regarding knowledge and behavior. These may be issues that are important to humans. And perhaps we may be able to go beyond personal opinion and preference, and address these in a scholarly way. However, even if important and scholarly, in the content of science policy one might ask whether the humanities deserve a place in our universities.

Do we need scholarly research and courses of studies in the humanities? A 2018 contribution to the *Chronicle of Higher Education* was titled "There Is No Case for the Humanities, and Deep Down We Know Our Justifications for It Are Hollow." Another title, a few months later: "The Humanities as We Know Them Are Doomed. Now What?" But one should not be misled by the titles humanities scholars give to their own critical reflections upon the humanities, as they do so in order to envisage possibilities in our current landscape and advocate a view of what the humanities are or should be.[1]

1 Justin Stover, "There Is No Case for the Humanities." *American Affairs* 1 (4), 210–224; reprinted with the subtitle "And Deep Down We Know Our Justifications for It Are Hollow," *The Chronicle of Higher Education*, March 4, 2018; Eric Hayot, "The

Policies and possibilities in the current landscape differ from country to country and from discipline to discipline. Concerns regard student numbers, academics without tenure, the job market for graduates, freedom of speech and political bias, and cuts in programs and budgets. With this book, I intend to address an underlying issue by offering a view of what the humanities might be. In this concluding chapter, I will consider arguments for the importance of the humanities. Before turning to those arguments, there are two issues about humanities in higher education and research that might be worth clarifying in advance.

Research is often the central focus of science policy. Increasingly, funding for research is framed in the context of an even larger domain, social sciences and humanities, SSH. This comes with an interest in addressing societal challenges related to migration, urbanization, health, the societal impact of big data, and so on. These societal challenges are addressed best, so it is assumed, by combining sociology, psychology, and related behavioral disciplines with law, economics, and humanities. With the focus on problem solving comes a particular discourse on science policy, focusing on the products of scientific and scholarly research, on innovation and impact.

Some of the reflections on the humanities offered here, can be applied well to this larger SSH domain. However, interest in the way humans understand the world, others, and thus the cultural dynamics, implies that contributions that by scholars in the humanities will be different from those made by colleagues in economics, law, and social and behavioral sciences. Humans are not merely economic agents, members of social groups, factors to be taken into account in the dynamics of society. We are actors, who act for reasons. And not only are we actors in our actions, but we are also actors as readers of literature and of text messages, viewers of advertisements and abstract art, as perception is not merely reception, but also interpretation. We are persons who have an inner life that shapes how we experience the

Humanities as We Know Them Are Doomed. So What?," *The Chronicle of Higher Education*, July 1, 2018; a longer version in the online journal of the Modern Language Association, MLA, as "The Sky Is Falling," *The Profession*, May 2018. A defense is the report *The Heart of the Matter: The Humanities and the Social Sciences for a Vibrant, Competitive, and Secure Nation* (Cambridge, MA: American Academy of Arts and Sciences, 2013).

world and act within it. Given this self-involving character, the vocabulary of "knowledge production" is not fully adequate when applied to the humanities, as we will see below. Nonetheless, the humanities are not exempt from policy considerations and public accountability, nor should those involved keep themselves aloof of such mundane issues. Humanities scholars also need to earn their salaries. They too, desire to be relevant in some way, and often are more relevant than simplistic science policy discourse might display.

When it comes to *education*, there are two different settings for education in the humanities, one customary in the USA, the other in Europe. In the USA, after completing high school students might go to a college that offers a broad bachelor program. Within such a liberal arts and sciences program, students may be required to take courses in different domains, including some in the humanities. In later years, they choose an area of concentration, a major, such as English literature, religious studies, physics, psychology, or some other discipline. There are graduate programs offering various master degrees and doctorates, but for many the next stage of higher education has a professional orientation, in a law school, a medical school, a business school, a school of engineering, at a teacher's college or in a seminary or divinity school. Some would prefer to see such a more specific orientation already in the undergraduate stage. But, as Michael S. Roth has advocated, we should not give in to the push for vocational undergraduate programs. Such a move would neglect "a deep American tradition of humanistic education that has been integral to our success as a nation and that has enriched the lives of generations of students by enhancing their capacities for shaping themselves and reinventing the world they will inhabit."[2]

In European countries, the course of studies is often disciplinary right from the start, envisaged mostly as providing a fundamental base of knowledge and skills, rather than as vocational training. Thus, after high school the students go to university to study English literature, Middle Eastern studies, philosophy, psychology or physics, but also programs with a more professional orientation, such as law, medicine, or business. Some do electives outside their chosen field of studies, but

2 Michael S. Roth, *Beyond the University: Why Liberal Education Matters* (New Haven, CT: Yale University Press, 2014), p. 3.

the core of their education concentrates on a discipline or domain. This second model gives priority to the development of expertise in a discipline or subject area, whereas the liberal arts and sciences model emphasizes general analytical and presentation skills, "critical thinking." In recent decades, some universities in Europe, including almost all in the Netherlands, have introduced, alongside their disciplinary programs, liberal arts and sciences programs, often framed as internationally oriented, English language "university colleges."

Among arguments for the relevance of the humanities, we may distinguish various types, focusing on the humanities as driven by the quest for fundamental knowledge (which might become useful in a distant future), on the humanities as knowledge that is useful for business or contributes to public value, and on the humanities as a pursuit that is valuable in itself, as a reflection of who we are, humans.

HUMANITIES PRODUCE FUNDAMENTAL KNOWLEDGE

Fundamental science works best if it is not directly profit-oriented. One needs a place where imagination can run freely, where there is patience to allow for research that might show its relevance and usefulness in unanticipated ways, perhaps only centuries later. That, at least, is the vision offered in *The Usefulness of Useless Knowledge* by the founding director of the Princeton-based Institute of Advanced Studies, Abraham Flexner, and his current successor, Robert Dijkgraaf. This Institute for Advanced Studies is a top institute in mathematics and physics, while its schools for social sciences and history should also not be underestimated, as the founding professor for the school of social sciences was Clifford Geertz, while Jonathan Israel is an emeritus professor of its school of historical studies, to refer to two scholars referred to in previous chapters.[3]

Emphasis on fundamental scholarship animates Rens Bod's *New History of the Humanities*. Discoveries in the grammar of Sanskrit by the Indian grammarian Panini, well over two-thousand years ago,

3 Abraham Flexner, *The Usefulness of Useless Knowledge*, with a companion essay by Robert Dijkgraaf (Princeton University Press, 2017).

found their application in computer languages, millennia later. Curiosity-driven research should indeed be driven by curiosity, by questions that the scholars themselves come up with. Requiring short-term relevance would be a poor guiding principle for academic policy. Fundamental research, also in the humanities, may become useful *because* it provides insight into fundamental patterns. The focus should be on the knowledge itself, not on its application.[4]

I consider this an important and valid argument for fundamental research in the sciences and in the humanities. But the argument seems to work best for research that is most similar in kind to research in fundamental natural sciences, the search for underlying laws and theories. In the case of the humanities, the search for patterns thus might take precedence over more interpretative, critical, and reflexive approaches. While I agree that we should think about the humanities and other sciences as fundamental disciplines, driven by curiosity, such curiosity can roam broader than the pattern-seeking type of humanities, as curiosity might also concern particulars and human motives that could become our own. Also, while I share the emphasis on the intrinsic value of the humanities as knowledge, there are other arguments – for the sciences and the humanities – that are relevant too. Just as the natural sciences are useful, as clearly visible in engineering and health care, so too can the humanities be useful, both commercially and as a contributor to public value.

HUMANITIES ARE USEFUL

Business interests make some of the humanities very useful. In 2013, the chairman of the Dutch association of employers said that we in the Netherlands should make the acquisition of skills in German obligatory in secondary education, as Germany is our most important trade partner.[5] Appropriate language skills are good for business. Similar arguments might be put forward for the study of Chinese, Korean, Japanese, and of languages and cultures of emerging economies. Other work carried out in the humanities may have commercial value itself,

4 Rens Bod, *A New History of the Humanities: The Search for Patterns and Principles from Antiquity to the Present* (Oxford University Press, 2013).

5 Bernard Wientjes, 2013; duitslandinstituut.nl/artikel/3017/knokken-voor-duits-op-rocs.

e.g. research and development in business communication, automatic translation, and gaming.

The business side of the humanities is broader than people might at first sight imagine. Leiden, a Dutch university town, not only has a Bioscience Park where one finds the science laboratories of the university and a wide range of high-tech companies. The economy of the old town is shaped by the humanities, with museums, publishers, translation services, specialized travel agents, services for design and editing, and many more small businesses that have their roots in humanities scholarship. According to a report from 2013, the humanities business in Leiden is larger than science-based business; in terms of companies 34 percent versus 7 percent; in terms of staff 34 percent versus 22 percent. Thus, it might be every euro invested in the humanities could yield multiple euros as return on investment.[6]

A similar argument about the job market may be brought forward with respect to a student's choice for humanities as a course of studies, thinking of future jobs. The linguist Joseph Aoun, President of Northeastern University in Boston, envisages that we need a "humanics" program where students acquire data literacy, technological literacy, and human literacy, while also having various cognitive capacities, including *cultural agility* and *critical thinking*; he holds that this is what employers want.[7] Whether with a fancy new name such as "humanics" or not, such programs are already emerging, often as interdisciplinary humanities programs.

In *You Can Do Anything: The Surprising Power of a "Useless" Liberal Arts Education*, George Anders argues that a humanities major opens the door to many jobs that come into being due to modern technology, jobs that don't exist yet. A humanities education may stimulate creativity, curiosity, critical thinking, empathy, international competence, listening, reading, and writing. Emotional intelligence, communication skills, and the ability to live with ambiguity are essential in a complex, dynamic, and globalizing world. "The job market is

6 Margreet Steiner and Eric Went (eds.), *Alfa's van Leiden: Creatief, ondernemend én succesvol* (Leiden: Stichting Leiden Communicatiestad, 2013), p. 8. They used a broad understanding of humanities that included archeology, anthropology, political sciences, and law.

7 Joseph E. Aoun, *Robot-Proof: Higher Education in the Age of Artificial Intelligence* (Cambridge, MA: MIT Press, 2017).

quietly creating thousands of openings a week for people who can bring a humanist's grace to our rapidly evolving high-tech future." He expects that the fastest growth is in jobs that relate *indirectly* to technological developments. A liberal arts student with a major in the humanities may thus land a crucial job inside companies who deal with the interplay of *technology and people*, whether it is finance, government, nonprofits, creative industry, health, training, or virtual reality. Or they might become entrepreneurs, perhaps delivering to people services or goods not yet envisaged.[8] Of course, creativity, curiosity, and critical thinking alone are not delivering a job market that gives the same opportunities to all, as the whole process, from admissions to the hiring of graduates, might be skewed in such a way that education reproduces a socio-economic elite. But that is more about the organization of schools, the funding of higher education, and bias in the credit given to graduates from different institutions, than about the disciplines themselves, whether humanities or a professional program in law or business.[9]

In his *Why We Need the Humanities: Life Science, Law, and the Common Good*, legal scholar and biotech entrepreneur Donald Drakeman argues that those who are not professionally involved in the humanities should support the humanities, as these are of central importance to our economic and political lives, to economic value (in his case, via the life sciences) and to public value, in his case, the legal sphere. He analyzes in some detail the pharmaceutical domain, where "ostensibly scientific and medical decisions are, in fact, based on very difficult, and largely unresolved, issues of distributive justice, fairness and the nature of the common good – questions that historically have been the province of the humanities." Private investments in the development of new drugs depend on public funds and arrangements), at the beginning of the process (basic research) and when the drugs go to market (health care funding and regulations). There is a much

8 George Anders, *You Can Do Anything: The Surprising Power of a "Useless" Liberal Arts Education* (New York: Little, Brown and Company, 2017), p. 4.

9 On elite schools in the US and the reproduction of the elite: William Deresiewicz, *Excellent Sheep: The Miseducation of the American Elite and the Way to a Meaningful Life* (New York: Free Press, 2014).

broader "public sphere" within which the technological and scientific development has its place and bears its fruits.[10]

PUBLIC VALUE

The humanities may be useful economically, providing skills needed for jobs. However, framing issues regarding science policy in such terms, arguing for a positive "return of investment," treating research as useful problem solving, and counting impact in terms of exploitable patents, technology transfer, and commercially marketable outcomes, relies upon a rather shallow and naïve view of what a society is.[11] A society is not a business, where in the end, net profit counts. It is more like a household, a group of people who have multiple interests of various kinds, some shared and some different, that need to be combined as far as possible, in a way that is reasonable and fair to all members of that household. Etymologically, even the term "economy" has such a connotation, as it is associated with Greek words, as the management (*nemomai*) of the *oikos*, of the house. In that light, economic usefulness is about more than profit in businesses and lucrative jobs for individuals. It is about society as the human household. Though there may be private and commercial benefits, this emphasis on society, on collective interests, seems to me a natural context for justifying the humanities, as contributor to public value for humanity.

An interesting collection of essays initiated by the Arts and Humanities Council (UK) is *The Public Value of the Humanities*, edited by Jonathan Bate.[12] The contributions are grouped into four rubrics:

- o Learning from the past,
- o Looking around us,
- o Informing policy, and
- o Using words, thinking hard.

10 Donald Drakeman, *Why We Need the Humanities: Life Science, Law and the Common Good* (Houndmills, Basingstoke: Palgrave Macmillan, 2016), p. 9.

11 Paul Benneworth, Magnus Gulbrandsen, and Ellen Hazelkorn, *The Impact and Future of Arts and Humanities Research* (London: Palgrave Macmillan, 2016), chapter 1.

12 Jonathan Bate (ed.), *The Public Value of the Humanities* (London: Bloomsbury, 2011).

We may learn from others, past and present, near and far. Such lessons may inform policy, but so, too, might be the analysis of arguments and of the way terms are used. This is also the message of *The Humanities and Public Life*, edited by Peter Brooks and Hilary Jewett, in which the contributors emphasize "the ethics of reading," and its relevance for many professions.[13] The ethics of reading involves ethics in the selection of the texts professionals use but also a broader sensibility to language, to human lives and the need for interpretation, developed by reading literature. In this context, it may be noteworthy to consider the extent to which historical and philosophical literature plays a role in the reasoning of the justices of the Supreme Court in the USA, and more generally in legal practice.[14] Abuse of language may have real consequences, and so, positively, may a well-developed sense of reading, sensitive to context and genre, respectful of ambiguity and uncertainty if appropriate to the situation, be important to public life and to professionals of many different kinds.

In the framework program of the European Union on research funding for the period 2014–2020, *Horizon 2020*, societal challenges are a prominent category in the funding programs, and they will be again for the next seven-year period. The challenges included health, agriculture, energy, transport, and climate as areas where principal investigators may come from engineering and life sciences, but also "Europe in a changing world – inclusive, innovative and reflective societies" and "Secure societies – protecting freedom and security of Europe and its citizens." With epithets such as "inclusive, innovative and reflective," issues of cultural diversity, inclusion and exclusion are on the table, while the addition of freedom of citizens and protection of their security also has the potential of going beyond an all too straightforward legal or surveillance discourse. As with pure research, it may be difficult for societal challenges to anticipate what will be most useful, as unexpected political developments may create unanticipated needs for cultural expertise. Such expertise might be relevant in many different contexts, including those that may at first be

13 Peter Brooks and Hilary Jewett (eds.), *The Humanities and Public Life* (New York: Fordham University Press, 2014).

14 Drakeman, *Why We Need the Humanities*, chapter 3.

understood mainly in engineering terms. Environmental policy depends not only on science, such as provided by the International Panel on Climate Change, but also on worldviews and culture; cleaning the Ganges in India requires understanding religious practices and beliefs.

I do agree that in the context of such science policy, the humanities and social sciences are important, if we want to come up with adequate ways to address those societal challenges. But arguing for the humanities within the context of such science policy agenda's may not do full justice to the humanities as such. From a humanities perspective, there might be ambivalent feelings about the language of science policy, and thus a desire to consider its limitations. Speaking of "products of research" or "deliverables" evokes the image of things that are countable, portable, and marketable. Speaking of "knowledge production" evokes the image of the division of labor in the factory, the image of a pipeline from invention to application, but do such images do justice to the explorative, creative dimension of research, also in the sciences? It may be even more ill-suited for work in the humanities that may be considered "destructive" rather than productive, or rather, to use more positive vocabulary, contributions from the humanities that are critical and challenging for existing beliefs and power structures. Besides, emphasis on production suggests that it is clear what is to be produced, but results of research are not really known before the work is done. Even less so when we are talking about ideas rather than things; if we have the idea we are looking for, we already have that idea. The language of "innovation" has its strength and weaknesses, too. What about care, curation for our heritage? What about criticism, challenging, raising questions, undermining answers? What about emancipatory engagement, not merely adding new gadgets to our repertoire, but changing social relations. "Innovation" sounds like the research and development language of businesses and patents. "Impact" has become the terminology of choice. It is broader, more open to non-commercial impact, and hence more suitable for articulating public value. However, when in science policy one seeks to assess research impact, it is too easily envisaged as something that could be done in a way that suits bureaucratic purposes, focusing on output, preferably countable and attributable to individual scholars or teams, competing with other teams or individuals.[15] Even the discourse about "public value," by using the singular "value," suggests something measurable, as a currency that can be counted across various contexts, whereas a plural "values" would evoke a deeper sense of pluralism, and perhaps even incommensurability, across domains, or of the impossibility of ever completing what it means to be human.[16]

Humanities enrich culture. At least, so one might argue, thereby making the emphasis on public value more specific by associating it with "high culture." Helen Small, in her book *The Value of the Humanities*, gives serious consideration to the argument that the humanities "contribute to happiness," individually or collectively. As she writes, "an educated familiarity with the range and depth and variety of human emotions and ways of understanding then constitutes one of the goods of education." Also, not only through education; the humanities may stimulate the arts and letters; they may contribute to the preservation of cultural heritage. Historians deepen our understanding of history, nationally, locally, and globally.[17]

This argument risks conflating the significance of literature, music, and art with scholarship on such human self-expressions. Human culture would be far less rich if there had not been great composers, playwrights, novelists, and poets; their works may inspire, nourish empathy, engage the imagination, satisfy a longing for beauty, or disturb us by the presentation of tragic features of existence. But did Bach or Mozart, Shakespeare, or Ibsen need the humanities? The question is anachronistic, as the humanities were not yet well-defined disciplines centuries ago.

15 Benneworth, Gulbrandsen, and Hazelkorn, *The Impact and Future of Arts and Humanities Research*, chapter 6. Also, the essays of "Part I The Humanities and Their 'Impact'" and "Part II Utility v. Value" in Eleonora Belfiore and Anna Upchurch (eds.), *Humanities in the Twenty-First Century: Beyond Utility and Markets* (Houndmills, Basingstoke: Palgrave Macmillan, 2013).

16 Incommensurability and the plurality of values: Inspired by Michael Bérubé, "Value and Values," in Michael Bérubé and Jennifer Ruth, *The Humanities, Higher Education, and Academic Freedom: Three Necessary Arguments* (Houndmills, Basingstoke: Palgrave Macmillan, 2015), a book that is, above all, an argument against the widespread use of non-tenured faculty for teaching humanities courses, in particular in the USA.

17 Helen Small, *The Value of the Humanities* (Oxford University Press, 2013), p. 123.

Do we need the humanities to make sense of their cultural contributions? We certainly need musicians that are able to play difficult pieces of music, but do we also need musicologists? Great personal wisdom would be lost in a world without literature, but does this suffice to justify literary studies? Well, if we need trained musicians who can perform a piece in a way that is respectful to the intentions of the composer, we also need to develop historical expertise, on the composer, on the instruments available at that time, and so on. A musician may decide to perform a piece of early modern music in a way not informed by such historical knowledge. Such a performance may be creative, just as giving a new twist to a classic text would be. In such a context, the artist or reader creates a new reality. Even this reality is informed by knowledge when the creative artist deviates from what is available.

Academic reflection may seem counterproductive from the point of view of the recipient. Believers may be disturbed by academic religious studies. When enjoying a piece of music, historical knowledge might be a distraction. But experts, who invested intellectual attention in the study of music, literature, art, or other facets of culture, may open us to new ways of experiencing. Closing one's mind to genuine knowledge that may offer us alternative perspectives, limits us as recipients of great legacies of the past, and thereby diminishes culture. More generally speaking, given the way humans are influenced by the reflection on humanity, a deeper level of engagement with our languages and histories, may be expected to enrich culture and serve nuance.

However, sadly enough, historical claims and ideas about linguistic purity may also be used for nationalistic politics or identity politics, excluding others, appropriating history for a particular agenda, drawing boundaries where there are interactions. The study of cultural artefacts may also single out the products of a particular "high culture," as I did when referring to Bach, Mozart, Shakespeare, and Ibsen a few paragraphs ago. Neither of these approaches is appropriate for the humanities; the first would be partisan, loaded with values that do not strengthen the scholarly attitude (see Chapter 4). The second would pass by the insight that all humans are cultural beings (Chapter 6). Thus, we need to envisage the domain of the humanities not merely in terms of culture in the sense of Western art and literature, but see it as much broader and pluralistic, with awareness of the many inhomogeneities and diversity of diversities within human existence.

Democracy needs the humanities, at least, according to Martha Nussbaum's *Not for Profit* (2010). The humanities should educate young people to become critical thinkers who can challenge customary beliefs and practices. The archetypical example is Socrates, the Greek philosopher who was condemned to death for corrupting the young people of Athens, by showing them the unsettling character of critical questions. A biblical association might be to see the scholar as a prophet; Small uses a less appealing figure when she speaks of "the gadfly argument."

According to Nussbaum, a humanities education might help students to develop empathy to appreciate the perspectives of others, to spot abuse of language and of power, and to engage in civil disagreement and hence political discourse. Much is at stake, as she argues in the opening sentences of her book:

> We are in the midst of a crisis of massive proportions and grave global significance. (. . .) I mean a crisis that goes largely unnoticed, like a cancer; a crisis that is likely to be, in the long run, far more damaging to the future of democratic self-government: a world-wide crisis in education.
>
> Radical changes are occurring in what democratic societies teach the young, and these changes have not been well thought through. Thirsty for national profit, nations, and their systems of education, are heedlessly discarding skills that are needed to keep democracies alive. If this trend continues, nations all over the world will soon be producing generations of useful machines, rather than complete citizens who can think for themselves, criticize tradition, and understand the significance of another person's sufferings and achievements. The future of the world's democracies hangs in the balance.
>
> What are these radical changes? The humanities and the arts are being cut away, in both primary/secondary and college/university education, in virtually every nation in the world. Seen by policy-makers as useless frills, at a time when nations must cut away all useless things in order to stay competitive in the global market, they are rapidly losing their place in curricula, and also in the minds and hearts of parents and children.

Though articulating a similar concern, Geoffrey Galt Harpham is more self-critical about the humanities, as these disciplines have also contributed to racism, colonialism, and elitism.[18] The claim that democracy needs the humanities might fit most easily for the Liberal Arts orientation, where humanities courses are part of a broader educational program for all students.

The democracy argument advocated by Nussbaum is sympathetic, as she advocates values that her readers are likely to share, such as a fairer distribution of opportunities and an understanding of a good life that involves more than merely economic prosperity, while addressing gross inequalities in the USA and in India. Her message may have acquired even greater urgency in the USA in the years since 2010 when the book was published. But are the humanities as scholarly disciplines necessary for democracy? In complex societies literacy is essential, as is a well-informed informed general public, people who can evaluate merits of arguments. This may require training teachers and others involved in public outreach. Would it also justify scholarly research and higher education in the humanities?

One concern is that claiming a particular moral or social role for academic humanities seems to neglect the democratic importance of all citizens. The claim that the humanities are necessary, passes by exemplary moral contributions made by people with other disciplinary backgrounds, such as economists addressing inequality (e.g., Jan Tinbergen, Amartya Sen), physicists who stood up for civil liberties and responsibility (e.g., Andrei Sakharov and the Pugwash Conferences on Science and World Affairs), and doctors working to make medical aid available worldwide (e.g., *Médecins Sans Frontières, Doctors without borders*). Also, not only in practice; careful and critical reflections on economic ideas have come from economists, and so, too, for other disciplinary domains. Competence in the humanities need not even deliver the political goods intended; an ethicist need not be particularly ethical, just as a barber may well

18 Martha Nussbaum, *Not for Profit: Why Democracy Needs the Humanities* (Princeton University Press, 2010), pp. 1–2; "Gadfly Argument" is in the title of Small's fourth chapter. Geoffrey Galt Harpham, *The Humanities and the Dream of America* (University of Chicago Press, 2011), p. 96.

be bald.[19] The humanities even have disadvantages, as humanities scholars may be so well-versed in language and argumentation that a discussion on a moderate issue of policy develops into a major battle over methods and worldviews or into an overly skeptical outlook.

Thus, *Democracy needs the humanities* might be an overstatement. However, a complex democratic society is served well by citizens who have the ability to engage in careful reflection on their own understanding of humans and of the world, and a citizenship that is informed about minorities and about diversity within minority groups, and much else, a world in which we learn to understand others, and are aware of the potential for bias involved in the process. Thus, a climate that allows for the intellectual and personal efforts typical of the humanities, is conducive to democracy, though in the end, democracy is up to citizens, those with training in the humanities and those without. Accessible and stimulating primary and secondary education is far more important than academic humanities, though the humanities may contribute to the quality of such education.

USEFULNESS AND PUBLIC VALUE NEED MORE

Training humanities students who might become teachers, journalists, researchers for NGOs, religious leaders, or civil servants, is a major contribution to the diversity of professions we need. However, such a consideration seems not to reach very far. That it is good for business that Dutch students learn German reasonably well does not work as an argument for the academic study of Middle High German, German idealist poetry, or of relations within the Indo-European language family. Or so it seems. Actually, the pragmatic interest in expertise on German does provide a basis for a broader ambition.

A teacher needs more than a teacher needs. We need teachers who can train people to analyze well and express themselves clearly and eloquently. These do not need to turn all civilized speakers into linguists. Hence, one might assume, we could limit our work to instrumental purposes, to what is useful, training teachers who are

19 Stefan Collini, *What Are Universities For?* (London: Penguin, 2012), p. 98f, expresses similar concerns about Nussbaum's position. The analogy of the bald barber I owe to the late Paul van Dijk, who taught ethics at Twente University, the Netherlands.

competent enough to teach. However, being human, teaching, and being taught, resists such narrow constraints. Someone learning German might notice similarities to Frisian, Dutch or English, and thus raise questions about the historical development of these languages. Training people to analyze a text well makes them raise questions about methods and criteria, and thus questions of a more academic nature.

If we want good teachers, they will need to have a broader basis than the immediate knowledge they need to have at their disposal in everyday practice. In their training, they not only need to acquire professional skills, but also a broader academic habitus and knowledge. This not only applies to teachers, but equally to those working on intercultural understanding, on heritage, on libraries and the data-driven society, on health communication, and much else. Furthermore, our students need more than the professional skills needed today because the world is changing rapidly; they will need to be prepared for positions that do not exist yet. Thus, to stay with the teacher as an example, the demand for teachers requires that teachers are themselves able to keep learning on such issues, and can be informed by specialists, including those dealing with particular issues in greater depth, uncovering complex histories, patterns, and meanings.[20]

HUMAN HUMANITIES

The humanities may be defended as useful and having public value. There is one more argument for the value of the humanities, an argument rooted in the understanding of humanities as being about human self-understanding and self-expression. Given that the work has been done in previous chapters, this argument that roots humanities in human nature, as *human humanities*, can be brief.

Humans are interestingly expressive and explorative in language and culture. Given the capacity for creative circularity that has arisen in human evolution, we also reflect upon ourselves and others, individually and collectively, familiar and strange. Thus, doing humanities

20 Similarly, Collini, *What Are Universities For?*, p. 56.

is intrinsic to humans, even for those who are not professionally involved in the humanities.

In *The Value of the Humanities*, Helen Small also argued for the importance of the humanities "for its own sake," developing an argument informed primarily by literary studies and historical scholarship. Stefan Collini announced early in a chapter on "The character of the humanities" that at the end of the chapter he will "directly address the vexed question of how best to go about 'defending' the humanities." When he gets there, he points, very briefly, to human life:

> The kinds of understanding and judgement exercised in the humanities are of a piece with the kinds of understanding and judgement involved in living a life. All we can say at this point is that *that*, in the end, is why they interest us and seem worthwhile.[21]

We, humans, espouse a great variety of values; not everyone needs to be professionally interested in pursuing the humanities in depth.[22] For some of us, this reflective effort becomes their professional course of studies. For many more, human self-reflection may take the form of curiosity about particular languages, histories, cultures, and religions. It may stimulate us to seek patterns across different forms of human behavior. Also, thinking of the moral connotation of "humanity," self-understanding as humans brings with it the obligation to seek to understand the other, to engage in dialogue across cultural distances of various kinds. All these activities contribute to a human and humane world. Thus, engaging in the human study of humans is human.

It is our nature to be reflective. We not only communicate but reflect on communication. We not only have a culture, we are always revising and creating culture. Thus, human humanities are natural to humans and necessary for the good of complex and quickly changing society. Not all reflection is academic, of course, but the study of humans is among the most human and humane things we humans can do.

21 Small, *The Value of the Humanities*, pp. 151–173; Collini, *What Are Universities For?*, pp. 62 and 85.

22 Susan Wolf, *The Variety of Values: Essays on Morality, Meaning, and Love* (Oxford University Press, 2015).

Selected Literature

Anders, George. 2017. *You Can Do Anything: The Surprising Power of a "Useless" Liberal Arts Education*. New York: Little, Brown and Co.

Aoun, Joseph E. 2017. *Robot-Proof: Higher Education in the Age of Artificial Intelligence*. Cambridge, MA: MIT Press.

Appadurai, Arjun. 1996. *Modernity at Large: Cultural Dimensions of Globalization*. Minneapolis, MN: Public Worlds.

Appiah, Kwame Anthony. 2018. *The Lies That Bind: Rethinking Identity*. London: Profile Books.

Bate, Jonathan (ed.). 2011. *The Public Value of the Humanities*. London: Bloomsbury.

Belfiore, Eleonora and Anna Upchurch (eds.). 2013, *Humanities in the Twenty-First Century: Beyond Utility and Markets*. Houndmills, Basingstoke: Palgrave Macmillan.

Benneworth, Paul, Magnus Gulbrandsen, and Ellen Hazelkorn. 2016. *The Impact and Future of Arts and Humanities Research*. London: Palgrave Macmillan.

Bérubé, Michael and Jennifer Ruth. 2015. *The Humanities, Higher Education, and Academic Freedom: Three Necessary Arguments*. Houndmills, Basingstoke: Palgrave Macmillan.

Bod, Rens. 2013. *A New History of the Humanities: The Search for Patterns and Principles from Antiquity to the Present*. Oxford University Press.

Brooks, Peter, with Hilary Jewett (ed.). 2014. *The Humanities and Public Life*. New York: Fordham University Press.

Collini, Stefan. 2010. *That's Offensive! Criticism, Identity, Respect*. London: Seagull.

2012. *What Are Universities For?* London: Penguin.

Deacon, Terrence. 1997. *The Symbolic Species: The Co-Evolution of Language and the Human Brain*. New York: Norton.

Deresiewicz, William. 2014. *Excellent Sheep: The Miseducation of the American Elite and the Way to a Meaningful Life*. New York: Free Press.

Drakeman, Donald. 2016. *Why We Need the Humanities: Life Science, Law and the Common Good.* Houndmills, Basingstoke: Palgrave Macmillan.

Felski, Rita. 2008. *Uses of Literature.* Malden, MA: Blackwell.

Fish, Stanley. 2014. *Versions of Academic Freedom: From Professionalism to Revolution.* University of Chicago Press.

Geertz, Clifford. 1973. *The Interpretation of Cultures.* New York: Basic Books.

Harpham, Geoffrey Galt. 2011. *The Humanities and the Dream of America.* University of Chicago Press.

Hollis, Martin. 1994. *The Philosophy of Social Science: An Introduction.* Cambridge University Press.

McCutcheon, Russell T. 1999. *The Insider/Outsider Problem in the Study of Religion.* London: Cassell.

Nussbaum, Martha. 2010. *Not for Profit: Why Society Needs the Humanities.* Princeton University Press.

Oreskes, Naomi, and Erik M. Conway. 2010. *Merchants of Doubt: How a Handful of Scientists Obscured the Truth on Issues from Tobacco Smoking to Global Warming.* New York: Bloomsbury.

Plessner, Helmuth. 2019. *The Levels of Organic Life and the Human: An Introduction to Philosophical Anthropology.* Translated by Millay Hyatt. New York: Fordham Press.

Roth, Michael S. 2014. *Beyond the University: Why Liberal Education Matters.* New Haven, CT: Yale University Press.

Sideris, Lisa H. 2017. *Consecrating Science: Wonder, Knowledge, and the Natural World.* Oakland, CA: University of California Press.

Small, Helen. 2013. *The Value of the Humanities.* Oxford University Press.

Wolf, Susan. 2015. *The Variety of Values.* Oxford University Press.

Index